Prophet Muhammad's Miracles

The Nineteenth Letter

Bediüzzaman
Said Nursi

Rutherford, New Jersey
2002

Copyright © 2002 by The Light, Inc.

&

Copyright © 2002 by Işık Yayınları

All rights reserved. No part of this book may be reproduced or transmitted in any form or by any means, electronic or mechanical, including photocopying, recording or by any information storage and retrieval system without permission in writing from the Publisher.

Published by The Light, Inc.

42 Park Ave.

Rutherford, NJ 07070 USA

www.thelightinc.com

contact@thelightinc.com

Library of Congress Cataloging-in-Publication
data available

Nursi, Said, 1873-1960.
Prophet Muhammad's miracles /
Bediuzzaman Said Nursi.
p. cm. -- (From the Risale-i nur collection)
Includes index.
ISBN 0-9720654-1-5 (pbk.)

Printed and bound in Turkey

Table of Contents

Bediüzzaman and the Risale-i Nur ii

THE NINETEENTH LETTER

Prophet Muhammad's Miracles

His miracles 4

[Why Muhammad was honored with miracles • Types of miracles (news of the past and the future) • Actual miracles transmitted through indisputable chains of transmission • Miracles occurring before (but related to) his birth • His coming predicted in earlier Scriptures • His character and person • The Qur'an: His greatest and eternal miracle • His existence is the greatest manifestation of God's Existence and Unity and of eternal happiness]

Appendix 1: Further remarks about the 212
           Prophet's greatness

[Fourteen droplets discussing how the Prophet's universal personality qualifies him to be the Seal of the Prophets]

Appendix 2: The miracle of splitting the moon 231

[Five points explaining the wisdom behind this miracle]

Appendix 3: Why only Prophet Muhammad 238
           was honored with the Ascension

[Seven reasons explaining this unique honor]

Appendix 4: About knowing the Prophet 245

[Nine decisive proofs in the Prophet's character and mission that prove the Creator's Existence and Oneness]

Index 258

Bediüzzaman and the Risale-i Nur

In the many dimensions of his lifetime of achievement, as well as in his personality and character, Bediüzzaman (1873-1960) was and, through his continuing influence, still is an important thinker and writer in the Muslim world. He represented in a most effective and profound way the intellectual, moral and spiritual strengths of Islam, evident in different degrees throughout its fourteen-century history. He lived for eighty-five years. He spent almost all of those years, overflowing with love and ardor for the cause of Islam, in a wise and measured activism based on sound reasoning and in the shade of the Qur'an and the Prophetic example.

Bediüzzaman lived in an age when materialism was at its peak and many crazed after communism, and the world was in great crisis. In that critical period, Bediüzzaman pointed people to the source of belief and inculcated in them a strong hope for a collective restoration. At a time when science and philosophy were used to mislead young generations into atheism, and nihilistic attitudes had a wide appeal, at a time when all this was done in the name of civilization, modernization and contemporary thinking and those who tried to resist them were subjected to the cruelest of persecutions, Bediüzzaman strove for the overall revival of a whole people, breathing into their minds whatever and spirits whatever is taught in the institutions of both modern and traditional education and of spiritual training.

Bediüzzaman had seen that modern unbelief originated from science and philosophy, not from ignorance as previously. He wrote that nature is the collection of Divine signs and therefore science and religion cannot be conflicting disciplines. Rather, they are two (apparently) different expressions of the same truth. Minds should be enlightened with sciences, while hearts need to be illumined by religion.

Bediüzzaman was not a writer in the usual sense of the word. He wrote his splendid work the *Risale-i Nur*, a collection exceeding 5,000 pages, because he had a mission: he struggled against the materialistic and atheistic trends of thought fed by science and philosophy and tried to present the truths of Islam to modern minds and hearts of every level of understanding. The *Risale-i Nur*, a modern commentary of the Qur'an, mainly concentrates on the existence and unity of God, the Resurrection, Prophethood, the Divine Scriptures primarily including the Qur'an, the invisible realms of existence, Divine Destiny and humanity's free will, worship, justice in human life, and humanity's place and duty among the creation.

In order to remove from people's minds and hearts the accumulated 'sediment' of false beliefs and conceptions and to purify them both intellectually and spiritually, Bediüzzaman writes forcefully and makes reiterations. He writes in neither an academic nor a didactic way; rather he appeals to feelings and aims to pour out his thoughts and ideas into people's hearts and minds in order to awaken them to belief and conviction.

This book is a selected section from the *Risale-i Nur* collection.

THE NINETEENTH LETTER

Prophet Muhammad's Miracles

(NOTE: All Traditions[1] related in this treatise are from memory, for I have no reference books to consult. If there are mistakes in the wording, please correct them or consider them as paraphrases. According to the prevailing opinion among Tradition scholars, such paraphrasing is permissible.)

---

[1] The Arabic word *hadith*, commonly translated into English as Tradition, literally means news, story, communication, or conversation, whether religious or secular, historical or recent. In the Qur'an, this words appears in religious (39:23, 68:44), secular or general (6:68), historical (20:9), and current or conversational (66:3) contexts. The Prophet used it in a similar sense, for example, when he said: "The best *hadith* is the Qur'an" (Bukhari). However, according to the *Muhaddithin* (Traditionists [scholars of Traditions]), the word stands for "what was transmitted on the Prophet's authority, his deeds, sayings, tacit approvals, or descriptions of his physical appearance." Jurists do not include this last item in their definition. (Tr.)

This treatise illustrates Muhammad's [2] miraculous Messengership through more than 300 miracles that he worked, and is a marvel for:

FIRST: Although this treatise covers more than 100 pages and is based on Traditions and narrations, I wrote it while in the countryside, working 2 or 3 hours a day. I finished it in 2 or 3 days, working only from memory.

SECOND: Despite its length, this treatise does not bore the scribes or lose any of its pleasantness in its readers' eyes. In fact, it has aroused such enthusiasm, even in some lazy scribes, that in these hard and distressing times as many as 70 copies have been hand-written in this neighborhood within a year.[3] Those aware of this treatise's

---

[2] In any publication dealing with Prophet Muhammad, his name or title is followed by "upon him be peace and blessings," to show our respect for him and because it is a religious duty. For his Companions and other illustrious Muslims: "May God be pleased with him (or her)" is used. However, as this might be distracting to non-Muslim readers, these phrases do not appear in this book, on the understanding that they are assumed and that no disrespect is intended. (Ed.)

[3] The *Nur* (Light) treatises were hand-copied secretly until 1950, because the government of that time treated religious people harshly and Islam with hostility. (Tr.)

distinction conclude that it must be a wonder coming from his Messengership's miraculousness.

In the copies hand-written by nine scribes, including one inexperienced and unaware of *tawafuq*,[4] the words referring to the Prophet were found to be arranged unintentionally beneath one another throughout the treatise. This is the same in the Fifth Part for the words referring to the Qur'an.

The fair-minded will not see this *tawafuq* as mere coincidence, but rather as a mysterious sign and a wonder derived from his miraculous Messengership. The essentials explained at the treatise's beginning are very important. The Prophetic Traditions related in it are all authentic, according to the Traditionists, and report the most established phenomena concerning his Messengership. To enumerate this treatise's usefulness, another one of the same length would be needed. Therefore we invite those who desire to discover its usefulness to read it.

— Said Nursi

---

[4] *Tawafuq:* God's arranging things and events so that His servants obtain a good effect, such as the unintentional arrangement of key words one beneath the other on a page or in the same place on different pages. (Tr.)

[Said Nursi sometimes draws attention to his writings. This is not done out of self-praise. Rather, as a Muslim guide and inspired scholar dedicated to explaining the pillars of Islamic belief, worship, and morality as well as to establishing them in people's minds and hearts, and being completely confident of the truth of what he writes, he follows a style required by guidance. We should keep this in mind, as well as the period during which he wrote—a very hard time during which Islam was severely attacked and Islamic activities were kept under strict control and banned. (Tr.)]

His miracles

In His name, glory be to Him.

There is nothing that
does not glorify Him with praise.

In the Name of God,
the Merciful, the Compassionate.

He has sent His Messenger with the guidance and the religion of truth, that He might uplift it above every religion. God suffices as a witness. Muhammad is God's Messenger. (48:28-29)

Since Muhammad's Prophethood is proved in the Nineteenth and Thirty-first Words, here we point out only some of the gleams of that great truth in 19 signs as an addendum.

FIRST SIGN: The universe's Owner and Master does everything with knowledge, controls every affair with wisdom, directs everything perfectly, regulates everything all-knowingly, and arranges everything in a way to display the purposes and uses He wills for them. As the One who creates knows, the One who knows will speak. Since He will speak, He will speak to those having consciousness, thought, and speech.

Since He will speak to such people, He will speak to humanity, whose nature and awareness are the most comprehensive of all conscious beings. Since He will speak to humanity, He will speak to those most perfect and worthy of address. Since He will speak to the one most perfect and worthy of address, of the highest morality and who will guide humanity, He will speak to Muhammad, who has the highest disposition and morality and is followed (most sincerely) by one-fifth of humanity.

Half of the globe has submitted to his spiritual rule, and his light's radiance has illumined humanity for more than 13 centuries. Believers, the illumined section of humanity, renew their oath of allegiance five times a day, pray for his happiness, invoke God's blessings upon him, and admire and love him. Given this, He will speak to Muhammad and make him His Messenger and humanity's guide. Indeed, He has done so.

SECOND SIGN: The Prophet declared his Prophethood and proved it by presenting Qur'an and nearly 1,000 miracles. Their occurrence is as certain as his declaration of Prophethood. Another proof is that the Qur'an states that the most obstinate unbelievers charged him with sorcery. Unable to deny the miracles, they called them sorcery to satisfy themselves or to mislead their followers.

Muhammad's miracles are so certain that the Traditionists confirmed and reported them unanimously. A miracle is the Creator of the universe's confirmation of his Prophethood and has the effect of: "You have spoken the truth." For example, if one claims in the ruler's presence that the ruler has appointed him to a particular position, the ruler's "Yes" is enough to prove the person's claim. Furthermore, if the ruler changes his usual practice and attitude at that person's request, this makes his claim firmer.

The Messenger claimed to be the Creator of the universe's envoy, and God, in turn, changed His unbroken order at his prayer and request so that the miracles would prove his claim. Some of his hundreds of miracles are water running from his fingers, splitting the moon with a gesture of his finger, having a tree draw close to him to confirm and bear witness to him, and feeding 200 or 300 people with only enough food for 2 or 3 people.

However, the evidence of his truthfulness and his Prophethood's proofs are not restricted to his miracles. In fact, all of his deeds and acts, words and behavior, moral conduct and manners, as well as character and appearance, prove his truthfulness and seriousness. Indeed, such people as 'Abdullah ibn al-Salam, a famous Jewish scholar of that time, believed in him at first sight, saying: "No lie can hide in this face, nor can any guile be found in it."

Profound scholars say that the evidences of his Prophethood and his miracles amount to about 1,000; in reality, however, this is only the beginning. Countless people have affirmed it in their own particular ways, and the Qur'an itself provides thousands of such proofs in addition to its own 40 aspects of miraculousness. Since Prophethood is a fact, and more than 100,000 persons have claimed it and worked miracles, Muhammad's Prophethood is established more securely than any other Prophet's Prophethood. All evidence, qualities, and attributes related to the other Messengers' Prophethood are found in a more perfect and comprehensive manner in the person of Prophet Muhammad. Given this, he must be far more worthy to be chosen as a Prophet.

THIRD SIGN: His miracles are very diverse. Since his Messengership is universal, he is distinguished by miracles connected with nearly all species of creation. When a glorified ruler's aide-de-camp enters a city bearing diverse gifts, a representative from each section of the population welcomes him happily and in its own language.

Likewise, when the Eternal Sovereign's supreme Messenger honored the universe as an envoy to humanity and came bearing the Creator's light of truth and spiritual gifts related to the truths of the universe, he was welcomed as the Prophet by each species—from mineral elements to plants, animals and human beings, and from the moon and sun to stars—each in its own language and bearing one of his miracles. It would require many volumes to mention all of his miracles. Pure-souled meticulous scholars have compiled many volumes concerning his Prophethood's proofs, so here we point out only briefly the main categories of those miracles unanimously accepted as authentic.

These proofs fall into two main categories. The first (*irhasat*) includes miraculous events before his birth, at his birth, and before he declared his Prophethood. The second category pertains to all other proofs and has two subcategories: the wonderful events after his death and those displayed during his Prophethood. This latter group is subdivided into proofs manifested in his own person, moral conduct, and perfect character, and those miracles concerned with the outer world. This second subgroup consists of miracles related to spirituality and the Qur'an, and those related to material reality and creation.

The latter category is subdivided further into miraculous events during his mission that either broke the unbelievers' recalcitrance or reinforced the believers' belief. This branch has 20 different kinds, each having many instances and having been, at least in meaning, confirmed unanimously (e.g., splitting the moon, water flowing from his fingers, satisfying many people with little food, and being addressed by animals, trees, and rocks). The second branch includes some future events that happened just as he foretold.[5]

FOURTH SIGN: The future events he foretold, through the Knower of the Unseen's instruction, are beyond counting. Since his true reports about preceding ages, Prophets, and their nations are mostly found in the Qur'an, here we point out only a few of his correct predictions concerning his Companions, Family, and community. To ensure a complete understanding of the subject, we explain six essentials as a prelude.

FIRST ESSENTIAL: The Prophet's every act and state bears witness to his Prophethood and faithfulness. But not all of them need to be miraculous, for he was sent by the All-Mighty as a human being to guide and lead human beings in

---

[5] Unfortunately, I could not write as I had intended, and so wrote as my heart dictated. I could not follow the order of this classification.

their collective affairs and individual deeds to happiness in both this world and the next, and to disclose the wonders of God's art and the works of His Power, each of which is a miracle although it appears to us as ordinary and familiar. If he were extraordinary in all of his acts, he could not guide human beings and instruct them through his acts, states, and attitudes.

Being supplied with some extraordinary phenomena to prove his Prophethood to obstinate unbelievers, he worked miracles when necessary. But his miracles were never such that people were forced to believe against their will, as that would annul human free will in this arena of test and trial. If this were not so, there would have been no choice, meaning that Abu Jahl would have believed as did Abu Bakr and that no one could have been held responsible, in this life and the next, for their deeds.

It is surprising that while so many people believed in him because they saw him perform a miracle, speak some words, or glimpsed his face, some people today go astray as if these thousands of proofs are not enough, although they reach us through authentic lines of transmission and have caused countless discerning people to accept Islam.

SECOND ESSENTIAL: The Messenger is a human being and so acts as a human being. He is also a Messenger of God and thus an interpreter and envoy of the All-Mighty.

His message is based on the two kinds of Divine revelation: explicit and implicit. In the case of explicit revelation, the Messenger merely interprets and announces —he has no share in its content. The Qur'an and those Sacred Traditions (*hadith qudsi*[6]) whose meaning and content belong to God exclusively but whose wording belongs to the Prophet, are included here. In the case of implicit revelation, the essence and origin of which is based on Divine revelation and inspiration, the Prophet is allowed to explain and describe them. When he does so, he relies either on direct revelation and inspiration or on his own insight. When giving his own interpretation, he either relies on the perceptive power bestowed upon him due to his Prophetic

---

[6] *Hadith Qudsi:* This is a specific category of sayings from the Prophet. The wording is the Prophet's, but the meaning belongs to God. (Tr.)

mission or speaks as a person conforming to his time's common usages, customs, and kinds of comprehension.

Thus not all details of every Prophetic Tradition are necessarily derived from pure Revelation, nor are the sublime signs of his Messengership to be sought in his human thoughts and transactions. Since some truths are revealed to him in a brief and abstract form, and he describes them through his insight and in accord with normal understanding, the metaphors, allegories, or ambiguities he uses may need explanation or interpretation.

Remember that the human mind can grasp some truths only through analogy. For example, once a loud noise was heard in the Prophet's presence. He said: "This is the noise of a rock that has been rolling downwards for 70 years and now has reached Hell's lowest depths." An hour later, news came that a notorious hypocrite who recently had reached the age of 70 had died and gone to Hell. This report showed the interpretation of the Prophet's eloquent parable.

THIRD ESSENTIAL: A Tradition related by many reliable authorities (*tawatur*) is indisputable and is of two kinds: obvious *tawatur* (a Tradition with numerous chains of transmission by reliable authorities) and *tawatur* with respect to meaning. This second one also has two kinds: those agreed upon by silence and those unanimously related by different people but with different words.

In the first case, a Tradition related in the presence of others without engendering any dispute or is met with silence enjoys an implied acceptance. If those remaining silent are interested in the narration and are known to be very sensitive to errors and lies, their silence implies acceptance with far more certainty. The second kind, *tawatur* with respect to meaning, occurs when an incident is related unanimously by different people but with different words, as this also implies its actual occurrence. In addition, a report with only one chain of transmission sometimes amounts to the degree of *tawatur* in certain conditions or through some external signs.

Most of the Prophet's miracles and his Prophethood's proofs fall into either category. Although a few are related through only one chain of transmitters, they can be regarded as certain as if related through *tawatur*, since they have been accepted by confirmed authorities. Among such authorities were those who memorized more than 100,000 Traditions, who were so God-conscious that for 50 years they performed the morning prayer with the night prayer's *wudu'* (ablution) (spending night awake in long vigils), and who compiled the six authentic books of Tradition.[7]

Any Tradition accepted after much scrutiny has the certainty of *tawatur*, even if it had only one chain of transmitters, for such people were so familiar with the Prophet's Traditions and exalted style that they could instantly spot and reject one false Tradition among 100 reports. Like an expert jeweler recognizes a pure diamond, they could not confuse other words with those of the Prophet. However, such meticulous authorities as Ibn al-Jawziya were so excessive in their criticism that they considered several authentic Traditions to be false. This does not mean that the meaning of every false wording is wrong; rather, it means that the wording does not belong to the Prophet.

---

[7] These are the books of Traditions compiled by Bukhari (d. 870), Muslim (d. 875), Abu Dawud (d. 888), Tirmidhi (d. 892), Ibn Maja (d. 886), and al-Nasa'i (d. 915). (Ed.)

Question: What is the benefit of relating every Tradition through a chain of transmitters, so that they say, even for a well-known incident: "It is related from so-and-so and from so-and-so, etc."?

Answer: This has many benefits, such as showing the consensus of the truthful and reliable narrators, meticulous Traditionists, as well as the unanimity of the discerning authorities mentioned. Also, it shows that each scholar in the chain puts his seal on its authenticity.

Question: Why were miracles not transmitted with as great an emphasis as the Shari'a's basic rules?

Answer: The Shari'a's rules are used by most people to guide their lives and are applicable to everyone. Miracles, on the other hand, do not need to be known to everyone and only need to be heard once. For example, some religious obligations (such as the funeral prayer) only need to be observed by a few people and not the entire community. In the same way, only some people need to know about the miracles. This is why a miracle, no matter how much firmer its establishment is than a Shari'a rule, is transmitted by only one or two narrators, while a Shari'a rule is transmitted by 10 or 20 people.

FOURTH ESSENTIAL: The Messenger predicted some future events that are recurring, as opposed to isolated events having a particular significance in human history. They also have numerous aspects, each of which is explained through a different Tradition. A reporter combines these aspects as if a single narration, thereby making the Tradition appear to be at variance with reality.

For example, many narrations about the Mahdi have different details and descriptions. But the truth of the matter is that God's Messenger, relying on Revelation, told of a Mahdi who would appear in every century to preserve believers' morale, prevent them from falling into despair over social upheavals, and secure their heart-felt devotion to members of the Prophet's Family (a most-illustrious lineage).[8] He foresaw a Mahdi in every century similar to the Great Mahdi promised for the end of time. The

---

[8] The Prophet's Family: The Prophet, Ali, Fatima, Hasan, and Husayn. These people are known as the *Ahl al-Bayt,* the Family (or People) of the House. The Prophet's wives are not included in this designation. (Tr.)

'Abbasid caliph al-Mahdi, for example, regarded as belonging to the Prophet's Family, had many of the Great Mahdi's characteristics. So, narrations about the Mahdi differ due to confusing the Great Mahdi's qualities with those great caliphs or saints who came before him.

FIFTH ESSENTIAL: Since only God knows the Unseen, The Prophet did not know it by himself. He told his Companions whatever God, the All-Mighty, related to him about the Unseen.

The All-Mighty is also All-Wise and All-Compassionate. Thus His Wisdom and Compassion require the veiling of most future events, for as people consider many of them unpleasant, any prior knowledge of them would be painful. This is why we do not know when we will die and why the misfortunes we will experience remain behind the veil of the Unseen.

Divine Wisdom and Compassion also require that the Prophet not know the details of what will happen to his household and Companions after his death because of his deep compassion and tender-heartedness.[9] Nevertheless the All-Mighty

---

[9] For example, God's Messenger once said to his wives: "I wish I knew which of you will take part in that event,"

had a Divine purpose for telling him about some of them, albeit not in all their tragic aspects. He communicated pleasant events to the Prophet, either in outline or in detail, which the Prophet then related to his Companions.

Finally, his tidings were transmitted accurately to our own era by the great Traditionists who were at the height of piety, justice, and truthfulness, and who trembled with fear at such specific warnings as: "Whoever intentionally lies about me should prepare for a dwelling in the Fire"[10] and *But who does greater wrong than one who lies against God?* (39:32).

SIXTH ESSENTIAL: Many history books and biographies describe the Prophet's behavior and characteristics. But most discuss his human nature, and thus ignore his spiritual persona and

---

which shows that he did not know that 'A'isha would participate in the Battle of Camel. If he had known, his love and affection for her would have been hurt. However, later on he was informed of this somehow and told 'Ali: "There probably will be a matter between you and 'A'isha. Treat her gently and return her to her abode safely."

[10] Jalal al-Din al-Suyuti, *Jami' al-Saghir*; related from 70 Companions.

his being's sacred nature, both of which are very sublime and illustrious. For, according to the rule of "the cause is like the doer," the rewards of all Muslims' prayers are added to the accounts of his perfections from the day he declared his Prophethood (until the end of time). Every day he receives countless invocations by Muslims as well as God's infinite mercy, which he draws in like measure.

Further, since he is creation's result and most perfect fruit, as well as the beloved and interpreter of the Creator of the universe, his true nature and true perfections cannot be contained in accounts of his recorded human qualities. Certainly the stature of one served by archangels Gabriel and Michael as aides-de-camp during the Battle of Badr cannot be sought in accounts of, for example, his bargaining over a the price of a horse.

To avoid falling into error, we must focus on his true nature and illustrious spiritual persona in his rank of Messengership. Otherwise we may risk showing him disrespect or entertain uncertainties about his persona.

Consider the following analogies: Suppose a planted date-stone sprouts and becomes a tall, fruitful tree growing upward and outward; or that a chick from an incubated peacock egg hatches, grows into a beautiful peacock, and, adorned with the Pen of Divine Power, grows bigger and prettier still. The date-stone and egg possess qualities, properties, and precisely balanced elements, but they are not as striking and significant as those of the tree and the peacock that grew from them.

Given this, while describing the date-stone's and the egg's qualities along with those of the tree and the peacock, each item's qualities must be distinguished so that anyone following the description may find it reasonable. If this is not done (e.g., claiming that one date-stone [and not the tree] produces thousands of dates, or that the egg is [already] the prince of birds), people will be led to contradiction and denial.

The human nature of God's Messenger may be likened to that date-stone or egg, but his true nature, illumined with the Prophetic mission, is like the Touba tree or the Royal Bird of Paradise. Moreover, His true nature continues to grow more and more perfect. Given this, when one thinks of that exalted person bargaining with a Bedouin in the marketplace, he should gaze upon his illustrious essential nature, the one who rode the Rafraf during the Ascension, left Gabriel behind, and reached the Divine Presence. Otherwise, one risks showing insufficient respect to or failing to convince one's earth-bound soul of his true nature.

FIFTH SIGN: We will mention several Prophetic Traditions that predict future events, as follows:

- The Prophet announced from the pulpit in the presence of his Companions: "My grandson Hasan is a noble one. Through him, God will reconcile two large hosts."[11] Forty years later, when the two largest Muslim armies faced each other, Hasan made peace with Mu'awiya and fulfilled this prediction.

- He told 'Ali: "You will fight the oath-breakers, the unjust, and the deviators,"[12] thereby predicting the battles of the Camel and Siffin and those fought against the Kharijites.[13] Once

---

[11] Bukhari, *Kitab al-Sulh*, 3:244; Ibn Hanbal, *Musnad*, 5:37.

[12] Hakim, *Mustadrak*, 3:139; Bayhaqi, *Dala'il al-Nubuwwa*, 6:414.

[13] The Kharijites held that those who commit a grave error or sin and do not repent sincerely are no longer Muslims. Mere profession is not enough, for belief must be accompanied by righteous deeds. They also considered jihad one of Islam's

when talking with Zubayr in good, affectionate terms, the Prophet told 'Ali: "Zubayr will fight you, but he will be in the wrong."[14]

- He told his wives: "One of you will lead a serious rebellion. Many around her will be killed, and Haw'ab's dogs will bark at her."[15] These were proved by 'Ali's battles against 'A'isha, Talha, and Zubayr during the Battle of the Camel; against Mu'awiya at Siffin; and against the Kharijites at Haroura and Nahrawan.

- The Prophet told 'Ali that 'Abd al-Rahman ibn Muljam al-Khariji, whom he knew, would stain Ali's beard with the blood of his own head.[16] In addition, he also mentioned a bodily

---

pillars, due to their belief that "enjoining good and forbidding evil" meant vindicating truth through the sword. Although wiped out during the first two Islamic centuries for their almost constant rebellion against established authority, they are found today in small pockets in Oman and northern and eastern Africa. (Ed.)

[14] Ibn Kathir, *al-Bidaya wa al-Nihaya*, 6:213; Hakim, ibid., 3:366.

[15] Bayhaqi, ibid., 6:405-410; Hakim, ibid., 3:120.

[16] Ibn Hanbal, *Musnad*, 1:102; Haythami, *Majma'*, 9:138; Hakim, ibid., 3:113.

mark possessed by the Kharijite Dhul-Thadya. When that man's corpse was found among the dead Kharijites, 'Ali showed it to others as a proof of the rightness of his cause, thus making the miracle public.[17]

- Umm Salama and others related that the Messenger prophesied Husayn's death at Taff (Karbala'),[18] a tragic event that occurred 50 years later. He also repeatedly predicted, with some details, that his Family would be subjected to killing and exile after his death.[19] All that he predicted came true.

QUESTION: 'Ali's extraordinary courage and knowledge, and his kinship with the Messenger, qualified him to be caliph. Why did Abu Bakr, 'Umar, and 'Uthman reign before him? And why did the Muslim community experience so much disorder during his caliphate?

ANSWER: A great saint descended from the Prophet's Family is reported to have said: "God's

---

[17] Bukhari, 9:22; Muslim, 7:745; Bayhaqi, *Dala'il*, 6:426.

[18] Ibn Hanbal, *Musnad*, 6:294; Haythami, *Majma'*, 9:188; Bayhaqi, ibid., 6:468.

[19] Hakim, 4:482; *al-Jami' al-Saghir*, no. 2558.

Messenger desired 'Ali's caliphate, but was informed through inspiration that God willed otherwise. Upon this, he abandoned his desire and submitted to God's Will."

One reason why God's Will differed must have been this: If 'Ali had become caliph right after the Prophet's death, a time when the Companions needed agreement and unity more than ever, there probably would have arisen, as happened during his caliphate, a tendency in persons and tribes to compete because of his pure, uncompromisingly fearless, heroic, and independent behavior and attitude, as well as his widely known courage. Such competition might have divided the believers.

Also, the young Muslim community, which spread rapidly through tribal and ethnic intermingling, gradually caused 73 sects to emerge, just as the Prophet predicted. Thus, in circumstances that foster internal conflict and turbulence, a person of 'Ali's courage and sagacity was needed, someone who enjoyed the force and esteem of the Hashimites and the Prophet's Family. By fighting every hardship, 'Ali filled the Prophet's prediction: "I fought for the Qur'an's revelation. You will fight for its correct explanation against its forced, false interpretation."[20]

In 'Ali's absence, the pomp of worldly kingdom probably would have led the Umayyads completely astray. But his presence and that of the Prophet's Family made the Umayyad leaders restrict themselves, preserve their standing before the Muslim community, and do their best (if not willingly) or at least encourage their subjects and followers to protect and propagate Islam's truths and principles and the Qur'an's commandments.

As a result, countless meticulous Muslim jurists, distinguished Traditionists, saints and pure people of piety emerged during their reign. If they had not faced the perfect piety, sainthood, and virtue of the Prophet's Family, they probably would have gone completely astray from the very beginning, as happened toward the end of both their and the 'Abbasids' rule.

QUESTION: Why did the caliphate not remain in the Prophet's Family, although its members were the most deserving?

---

[20] Ibn Hanbal, *Musnad*, 3:83; Haythami, *Majma'*, 9:133; Tirmidhi, 5:635.

Answer: Worldly kingdom is deceptive, and the Prophet's Family was appointed to preserve Islam's truths and the Qur'an's injunctions. In order not to be deceived by caliphate or kingdom, one should be either infallible like a Prophet or as extraordinarily pure-hearted as the four Rightly-Guided Caliphs,[21] the Umayyad caliph 'Umar ibn 'Abd al-'Aziz, or the 'Abbasid caliph al-Mahdi.

The Fatimids in Egypt, the al-Mohads in North Africa, and the Safawids in Persia all show that worldly kingdom is not suitable for the Prophet's Family, for it causes them to neglect their essential duty of protecting and serving Islam. When they refrained from worldly kingdom, they served Islam and the Qur'an brilliantly and successfully.

Consider the leading saints descended from Hasan, particularly the four most eminent (Hasan al-Kharaqani, Hayat ibn Qays al-Harrani, Shaykh Hasan al-Shadhezili, and especially 'Abd al-Qadir al-Jilani) and the Imams descending from Husayn, especially Zayn al-'Abidin and Ja'far al-

---

[21] The four Rightly-Guided Caliphs: The first four rulers after the Prophet's death, namely, Abu Bakr, 'Umar ibn al-Khattab, 'Uthman ibn 'Affan, and 'Ali ibn Abu Talib. (Ed.)

Sadiq. Each became a spiritual guide of the highest rank and, dispelling the dark clouds of wrongdoing, spread the Qur'an's light and Islam's truth. They showed themselves to be true heirs of the Prophet.

QUESTION: What was the Divine Wisdom behind the terrible and bloody upheavals, and why did Divine Compassion allow such things to happen to those Muslims who cannot have deserved them?

ANSWER: A strong spring rain activates and develops predispositions inherent in vegetables, seeds, and trees so that each will bloom and flourish in its own fashion and realize its natural function. In the same way, upheavals during the time of the Companions and their successors activated various talents. Many people rose to preserve Islam, fearing that it was in danger. Women and men shouldered a duty to be performed in the Muslim community and strove to fulfill it to the best of their ability. Each group performed a different function, such as striving to preserve the Prophetic Traditions, to protect the Shari'a, to maintain the Qur'an and the truths of belief, and so on. This caused many branches of the religious and natural sciences to flourish, as well as many people of learning to appear. The seeds of a brilliant civilization were scattered throughout the vast Muslim world, and half of the ancient world changed into "rose gardens." Nevertheless, "thorns" (deviant sects) also appeared in these rose gardens.

It was as if Divine Power shook that age with wrath, turned it over vigorously, and thus electrified all people of zeal. Activated by that movement's centrifugal force, large numbers of illustrious jurists, enlightened Traditionists, blessed memorizers of the Qur'an and Traditions, people of purity and chiefs of saints dispersed throughout the Muslim world. Thus Divine Power inspired Muslims with enthusiasm and awakened them to the Qur'an's treasures.

Now we return to our subject. The Messenger predicted thousands of events, all of which came true. Here we mention only a few. Most are agreed upon by the six most authentic books of Traditions, including the two most famous: *Sahih al-Bukhari* and *Sahih al-Muslim*. Many of these Traditions have the certainty of *tawatur* with respect to their meaning, while others, on account of verification by meticulous researchers, may be considered as certain as if narrated through *tawatur*. All are authentic.

- "You (the Companions) will defeat all your enemies and conquer Makka, Khaybar, Damascus, Jerusalem, Iraq, and Persia. You will share the treasures of the Persian and Byzantine rulers among yourselves."[22] These empires were the superpowers of their time. The Prophet did not say "I think" or "I guess"; rather, he said it as if he had seen it. He predicted this while he was in severest circumstances with a handful of followers due to pervasive hostility in and around Makka.

- "After my death, you should follow the way of Abu Bakr and 'Umar."[23] In other words, Abu Bakr and 'Umar would succeed him as caliphs and act so perfectly as to please God and His Messenger. He also said that Abu Bakr's reign would be short, but that 'Umar would reign for a longer time and make many conquests.

---

[22] Ibn Hanbal, *Musnad*, 3:83; 'Ali al-Qari', *Sharh al-Shifa'* (from Bukhari, Muslim, and others), 1:678-79.

[23] Hakim, 3:75; also related by Tirmidhi, Ibn Hanbal, Ibn Maja, and Bayhaqi.

- "Earth was laid out before me, and I was shown its remotest corners in the east and west. My nation will extend over whatever was laid out before me."[24]

- Before the Battle of Badr, he indicated the exact places where the polytheistic Qurayshi leaders would be killed, and said: "Abu Jahl will be killed here, 'Utba here, Umayya here," etc., and added: "I will kill Umayya ibn al-Khalaf."[25]

- He informed his Companions of what was happening during the Battle of Muta (near Damascus), as if watching it, even though it would take someone one month to reach it on foot. He said: "Zayd has taken the flag and been hit; now Ibn Rawaha has taken it and been hit; now Ja'far has taken it and been hit; now one of God's swords (i.e., Khalid) has taken it."[26] Two or three weeks later, Ya'la ibn

---

[24] Muslim, 4:2215; Hakim, 4:445; also related by Tirmidhi, Ibn Hanbal, and Ibn Maja.

[25] Muslim, no. 1779; Ibn Hanbal, 1:390; Qadi 'Iyad, *Shifa'*, 1:343; Hakim, 2:327.

[26] Bukhari, 5:182; Hakim, 3:298; Abu Nu'aym, *Dala'il al-Nubuwwa*, 2:529.

Munabbih returned from the battlefront. In his presence, the Prophet described the fighting in detail and Ya'la swore by God that everything had happened exactly as described.

- "The caliphate after me will last for 30 years and then be replaced by a biting monarchy.[27] This affair certainly began with Prophethood and as a mercy. Then it will be mercy and caliphate, after which it will change into a biting monarchy, and finally into iniquity and tyranny."[28] In other words: The caliphates of four Rightly-Guided Caliphs and the 6-month caliphate of Hasan, after which the caliphate became a monarchy, and then was transformed into tyranny and the corruption of his nation.

- "'Uthman will be killed while reading the Qur'an. God probably will dress him in a shirt, but they will want to remove it from him."[29]

---

[27] *Al-Jami' al-Saghir*, no. 3336; Ibn Hanbal, 4:273; Ibn Hibban, *Sahih*, 8:227; Abu Dawud, *Sunna*, 8; Tirmidhi, *Fitan*, 48.

[28] Ibid.

[29] Hakim, 3:100; Ibn Hanbal, 6:114; Tirmidhi, no. 2706; *Majma'*, 5:188.

By this he meant that 'Uthman would become caliph, his deposition would be sought, and that he would be martyred while reading the Qur'an.

- According to an authentic narration, when the Prophet was cupped, he ordered 'Abdullah ibn Zubayr to bury the blood. Upon learning that Ibn Zubayr had drunk it as a blessing, he said: "Woe unto the people for what will befall them because of you, and woe unto you for what will befall you because of the people."[30] Thus he prophesied that the courageous Ibn Zubayr would lead the Muslims and that they would face awful attacks so that people would suffer great disasters. Ibn Zubayr declared his caliphate in Makka during the Umayyads' rule and fought heroic battles against them, until finally Hajjaj the tyrant martyred him after a fierce battle.

- The Messenger foretold the founding of the Umayyad state and that most of its rulers,

---

[30] Hakim, 3:554; *al-Matalib al-'Aliya*, 4:21; Qadi 'Iyad, *Shifa' al-Sharif*, 1:339.

including Yazid and Walid, would be unjust.[31] He also foretold that Mu'awiya would rule the Muslims and advised him to be just and mild: "When you rule, act gently."[32] The Prophet also predicted the Abbasids' long rule after the Umayyads, saying: "The descendants of 'Abbas will appear with black flags and rule for many times longer than them (the Umayyads)."[33]

- He prophesied the dreadful destruction of Genghis Khan and Hulagu, which caused the 'Abbasid state to collapse: "Woe to the Arabs for the evil that has approached."[34]

- The Prophet said to Sa'd ibn Abi Waqqas, when the latter was gravely ill: "Hopefully you will be spared so that some may benefit

---

[31] *Al-Jami' al-Saghir*, no. 412, 2579; *Shifa'*, 1:338; related by Tirmidhi and Hakim.

[32] Ibn Hajar, *Matalib al-'Aliya*, 4085, related by Ibn Hanbal and Abu Ya'la.

[33] Ibn Hanbal, 3:216; Hakim, *al-Mustadrak*, 3:326; Bayhaqi, *Dala'il*, 6:513.

[34] Bukhari, *Kitab al-Fitan*, 9:60; Muslim, no. 2880; Hakim, 1:108.

through you and others be harmed through you,"³⁵ suggesting that Sa'd would be a great commander and make many conquests. While many would benefit from him by converting to Islam, many others would be harmed through him because he would destroy their states. Later on, Sa'd commanded the Muslim armies that destroyed Persia's Sassanid Empire and brought many peoples within the guidance of Islam.

- When Negus, the Abyssinian ruler who embraced Islam, died 7 years after the Prophet's migration, he told his Companions what had happened and prayed the funeral prayers for him. A week later, news arrived announcing the Negus' death on the very day it was announced by the Messenger.³⁶

- When the Messenger was on top of either Mount Uhud or Hira with his four closest friends, the mountain trembled. He said:

---

[35] Abu Nu'aym, *Hilyat al-Awliya'*, 1:94, also related by Bukhari and Muslim.

[36] Bukhari, 2:109; also related by Muslim, Ibn Malik, Abu Dawud, and Nasa'i.

"Steady, for on you are a Prophet, a truthful one (Abu Bakr) and martyrs ('Umar, 'Uthman, and 'Ali)."[37]

Now O miserable, unfeeling, and wretched one who says that Muhammad was a wise man and then closes your eyes to that sun of the truth! Of his 15 kinds of major miracles, so far you have heard only a tiny part of one kind—that which is related to his predictions having the certainty of *tawatur*. One who predicts even only one-hundredth of such future events with his own insight would have to be of the highest genius.

Even if we merely regarded him as a genius, as you do, could such a person with the insight of a hundred geniuses have perceived anything false or so far abase himself as to give false information? Not to heed the words of such a person concerning happiness in both worlds is pure stupidity.

SIXTH SIGN:

- The Messenger told his daughter Fatima: "You will be the first Family member to join

---

[37] Muslim, 4:1880; also related by Bukhari, Tirmidhi, Hakim, and Abu Dawud.

me (after my death)."[38] When she died 6 months later, his words proved true. He also said to Abu Dharr: "You will be expelled from here (Madina), will live alone and die alone."[39] What he said happened 20 years later.

- Once he woke up in Umm Haram's house (Anas ibn Malik's aunt) and said with a smile: "I dreamed that my community was fighting in the sea like kings sitting on thrones." Umm Haram asked: "Pray that I may be with them." He replied firmly: "You shall be."[40] Forty years later she accompanied her husband 'Ubada ibn Samit during the conquest of Cyprus. She died there, and her tomb remains a visited place.

- "The Thaqif tribe will produce a liar who claims Prophethood, as well as a bloodthirsty tyrant."[41] In other words, the notorious Mukh-

---

[38] Bukhari, 4:248; Muslim, 4:1904; Ibn Hanbal, 6:77, Bayhaqi, 7:164.

[39] *Shifa' al-Sharif*, 1:343, related by Ibn Hanbal, Ibn Hibban, and Ibn Kathir.

[40] *Al-Jami' al-Saghir*, 6:24, related by Bukhari, Muslim, Tirmidhi, among others.

[41] Hakim, 3:453, also related by Muslim, Ibn Hanbal, and Tirmidhi.

tar (who claimed Prophethood) and the criminal Hajjaj (who killed 100,000 people).

- "Constantinople (Istanbul) will be conquered (by my community). How blessed is the commander who conquers it, and how blessed his army."[42] Constantinople fell to Sultan Mehmed the Conqueror, who thereby attained a high spiritual rank, in 1453.

- "If religion were hung on the Pleiades, descendants of the Persians would reach it and get ahold of it,"[43] indicating Persia's matchless scholars and saints.

- "A scholar from the Quraysh will fill the parts of Earth with knowledge."[44] This refers to Imam Shafi'i, who founded one of Islam's four legal schools.

- "My community will be divided into 73 sects, and only one of them will be saved." When

---

[42] Bukhari, *Tarikh al-Saghir*, 139; Hakim, 4: 422, also Ibn Hanbal and Haythami.

[43] *Al-Lu'lu' wa al-Marjan,* 3:183, related by Bukhari, Muslim, and Tirmidhi.

[44] *Kashf al-Khafa'*, 2:53, related by Ibn Hanbal, Tayalisi, Ibn Hajar, and Bayhaqi.

asked who they were, he replied: "Those who follow me and my Companions," meaning the people of the Sunna and Community (Ahl al-Sunna wa al-Jama'a).[45]

- "The Qadariya are the Magians of this community,"[46] thereby predicting the Qadariya sect,[47] which would split into several branches and reject Destiny.

- He predicted several groups would split into many factions when he told 'Ali: "On account of you, as with Jesus, two groups will perish: One because of excessive love (for you), and the other because of excessive enmity (for you)."[48] Christians, due to their excessive love

---

[45] Ibn Hanbal, 2:332; also related by Abu Dawud, Ibn Maja, and Tirmidhi.

[46] *Al-Jami' al-Saghir,* 4:150, related by Abu Dawud, Hakim, and Ibn Maja.

[47] Appearing in the second Islamic century, they advocated free will, said people create their own good and evil conduct, and accepted causality as a necessary part of human conduct, thus rejecting Divine Destiny.

[48] Hakim, 3:123; also related by Ibn Hanbal, Ibn Hibban, and Bazzar.

for Jesus, transgressed the limits and regarded him as God's "son," while Jews went so far in their enmity as to deny his Prophethood and perfections. This refers to the Rafidites,[49] the Kharijites, and the Nasiba, extremist partisans of the Umayyads, respectively.

QUESTION: The Qur'an demands that we love the Prophet's Family, and the Prophet greatly encouraged this. The Shi'as' love for them may serve as an excuse, for people of love may be likened to people of intoxication. So why cannot the Shi'a, especially the Rafidites, benefit from their love? Why did the Prophet condemn them for their excessive love?

ANSWER: There are two kinds of love. The first is loving somebody as a means to attain true love, which is love for the Prophet's Family in the name of God and his Messenger. Such love increases one's love of the Prophet and becomes a means to love God Almighty. Thus it is lawful, its excess is harmless and not considered a transgression, and it does not call for reproach and enmity toward others.

---

[49] *Majma' al-Zawa'id*, 10:22; *Fath al-Rabbani*, 24:20; Nasa'i, *al-Khasa'is*, 3:19.

The second takes the means as its real object. Such people "forget" the Prophet and devote their love to 'Ali (the Rafidites) due to his heroic acts and perfections, and Hasan and Husayn due to their extraordinary virtues, regardless of whether they recognize God and His Prophet. This love is not a means to love God and His Messenger, and its excess leads to reproach and enmity toward others. The Rafidites' excessive love for 'Ali caused them to reject the caliphates of Abu Bakr and 'Umar, deny their perfections, and go astray. Such excessive and negative love causes spiritual ruin.

- "When Persian and Roman girls serve you, you will be exposed to internal conflicts and civil war. The wicked will come to power and prey on the good."[50] This came true after 30 years.

- "'Ali will conquer Khaybar."[51] As a miracle of the Prophet and beyond all expectation, the following day 'Ali reached the gate of Khaybar's fortress, used it as a shield, and finally conquered Khaybar. When he threw the gate aside

---

[50] Haythami, 10:237; *al-Jami' al-Saghir*, 813; *Shifa'*, 1:237; Ibn Hibban, 8:253.

[51] Bukhari, 5:171; Muslim, no. 2406; Ibn Hanbal, 5:333; Hakim, 3:109.

after the conquest, eight (another version says 40) strong men could not lift it.[52]

- "The Hour will not come before two parties (of Muslims) fight (each other), although they make the same claims,"[53] predicting the Battle of Siffin between 'Ali and Mu'awiya.

- "'Ammar will be killed by a rebellious group."[54] When 'Ammar was killed at Siffin, 'Ali mentioned this as evidence that Mu'awiya and his followers were rebels. However, Mu'awiya and 'Amr ibn al-'As interpreted it as: "The rebels are his murderers, not all of us."

- "Disorder will not appear (among my community) as long as 'Umar is alive."[55]

- When Sahl ibn 'Amr was taken prisoner before his conversion to Islam, 'Umar told the

---

[52] Suyuti, *Tarikh al-Khulafa'*, 164; Ibn Kathir, *al-Bidaya*, 4:189, also related by Hakim, Ibn Ishaq, and Bayhaqi.

[53] *Al-Jami' al-Saghir*, 6:174; related by Bukhari, Muslim, and Abu Dawud.

[54] Muslim, 4:2236; Bukhari, 1:122; related from about 30 Companions.

[55] Bayhaqi, 6:386; Muslim, 4:2218; also related by Bukhari.

Messenger: "Let me pull out his teeth, for his eloquent speech incites the Qurayshi unbelievers to fight us." The Messenger replied: "'Umar, maybe he will assume a position pleasing to you."[56] When the Prophet died, Sahl delivered an eloquent sermon in Makka to steady and console the grief-stricken Companions. Remarkably, this sermon was almost the same in meaning and wording as that delivered, at the same time and for the same purpose, by Abu Bakr in Madina.

- "I wonder (Suraqa), how it will be with you when you wear the two bracelets of Chosroes (the Persian king)."[57] Chosroes was defeated during the reign of 'Umar, who put the bracelets on Suraqa and said: "Praise be to God, Who took these off Chosroes and put them on Suraqa."[58] The Prophet also declared: "Once (the rule of) Chosroes (meaning the

---

[56] Hakim, 4:282; Ibn Hajar, *al-Isaba fi Tamyiz al-Sahaba*, 2:93; *Shifa'*, 1:344.

[57] Ibn Hajar, ibid., no. 3115; 'Ali al-Qari, *Sharh al-Shifa'*, 1:703.

[58] *Shifa'*, 1:344; also *al-Isaba*, no. 3115.

Sassanid dynasty) is gone, there will be no other Chosroes,"[59] (thus predicting the end of the Sassanid rule in Iran.)

- When the envoy of Chosroes (the Sassanid king during the Prophet's time) reached Madina, the Prophet told him: "Chosroes has been killed by his son Shirviya Parwiz."[60] After confirming this, the envoy (reported to be Firouz) accepted Islam.

- When God's Messenger was about to set out for the conquest of Makka, a secret letter sent by Khatib ibn Abi Balta'a was already on its way to the Quraysh. He sent 'Ali and Miqdad, telling them: "The letter-carrier is in such-and-such a place. Go and bring it." They did as he asked. When the Messenger asked Khatib why he had sent the letter, Khatib gave an excuse and was pardoned.[61]

---

[59] Muslim, 4:2236; also related by Bukhari, Tirmidhi, and Tabarani.

[60] 'Ali al-Qari, ibid, 1:700; *al-Jami' al-Saghir*, 875; Abu Nu'aym, 2:348.

[61] Bukhari, 5:184; Muslim, No. 2494; Ibn Hanbal, 1:80.

- God's Messenger prayed: "May he ('Utba ibn Abi Lahab) be devoured by one of the dogs of God."[62] Later on, this man was devoured by a lion while traveling to Yemen.

- After the conquest of Makka, Bilal al-Habashi stood on the Ka'ba's roof and called the people to prayer (*adhan*). Several Qurayshi leaders, namely, Abu Sufyan, 'Attab ibn Asid, and Harith ibn Hisham, were sitting together near the Ka'ba. 'Attab said: "My father is fortunate not to witness this moment." Harith asked contemptuously: "Could not Muhammad find someone other than this black crow to be the *mu'azzin*?" Abu Sufyan did not comment, saying: "I am afraid that he will come to know whatever I say, and so will say nothing. Even if no one informs him, the rocks of this Batha (i.e., Makka) will do so." Shortly thereafter, God's Messenger came to them and repeated their conversation word for word. At that very moment 'Attab and Harith embraced Islam.[63]

---

[62] *Shifa'*, 1:343; related by Hakim, Bayhaqi, and Ibn Ishaq.

[63] Ibn Hajar, *al-Matalib al-'Aliya*, 4366; Ibn Hisham, *Sira*, 2:413.

Now, those of you who do not recognize the Prophet! Consider that two stubborn Qurayshi leaders believed after witnessing only one miracle. Consider how far you have been ruined so that you are not convinced even after hearing hundreds of his miracles, like this one, that came through *tawatur*. But let's return to our subject.

- The Muslims captured 'Abbas during the Battle of Badr. When asked for ransom, 'Abbas said he had no money. God's Messenger said: "You left that amount of money with your wife Umm Fadl in such-and-such a place (he gave the exact amount of money and named the place)."[64] 'Abbas confirmed this: "Only the two of us knew this," and then attained perfect belief.

- Labid, a dangerous Jewish sorcerer, invented a strong and effective spell to harm the Prophet. Winding some hair around a comb, he bewitched it and threw it into a well. God's Messenger told some of his Companions,

---

[64] Haythami, *Majma' al-Zawa'id*, 6:85; related by Ibn Hanbal, Hakim, and Bayhaqi.

including 'Ali: "Go to such-and-such a well and remove the spell from it." They did so, and the Messenger's discomfort lessened as they unwound the hair.[65]

- Once when with some important Companions, including Abu Hurayra and Hudayfa, the Prophet mentioned the fate one of them would meet because of his later apostasy: "One of you will be in the Fire with a tooth bigger than Mount Uhud." Abu Hurayra would later relate: "I was so afraid, as only two members of that group remained. One of them was me. Finally, the other man was killed in the Battle of Yamama as an apostate in the company of Musaylima."[66]

- Before converting to Islam, 'Umayr and Safwan decided to kill the Prophet and collect a large reward. When 'Umayr came to Madina with this intention, God's Messenger summoned him, related the plot, and placed his

---

[65] Bukhari, 4:148; Muslim, 4:1719; Ibn Maja, 3545; Ibn Hanbal, 4:367.

[66] *Majma' al-Zawa'id*, 8:289; related by Tabarani and, with a slight difference, by Muslim; *Shifa'*, 1:342.

hand on 'Umayr's chest. 'Umayr confessed and became a Muslim.[67]

Many more of his predictions are recorded with chains of transmission in authentic books of Tradition. Most of the ones related here have the certainty of *tawatur* in meaning, being related in *al-Jami' al-Sahih* by Imam al-Bukhari and *al-Jami' al-Sahih* by Imam al-Muslim (commonly known as Bukhari and Muslim or *Sahih al-Bukhari* and *Sahih al-Muslim*, respectively), which are accepted by meticulous researchers as the most authentic sources after the Qur'an, and in the *Sunan al-Tirmidhi, Sunan al-Nasa'i, Sunan Abu Dawud, Musnad al-Hakim, Musnad al-Ahmad ibn Hanbal,* and *Dala'il al-Bayhaqi*.

Now then, you bewildered person, do not try to explain this away by calling Muhammad a wise man. His predictions, all of which have come (or will come) true, can be explained in only two ways. The first one is that he had such a keen sight and broad genius that he penetrated into all times and places and thereby learned of the past and the

---

[67] *Majma' al-Zawa'id*, 8:286; *Shifa'*, 1:342; Ibn Kathir, *al-Bidaya*, 3:313.

future. If someone had this quality, it would be no more than a wonder, a miraculous gift from the Creator of the universe, and one of the greatest miracles.

The second one is that he is an official instructed by a Being Who controls and observes everything, commands all times and places, and records everything in a great ledger. He then relates to His Messenger whatever and whenever He wills. Thus Muhammad instructs others as he is instructed by his Eternal Instructor.

- While appointing Khalid ibn al-Walid to fight against Ukaydir, the chief of Dawmat al-Jandal, the Prophet told him: "You will find him (Ukaydir) on a wild ox hunt," and that he would be captured without resistance.[68] Khalid found and captured Ukaydir in those exact circumstances.

- Some time after the Quraysh hung the leaf containing the articles of boycott against the Bani Hashim (the Prophet's clan) on the Ka'ba's wall, the Messenger told them: "Worms have

---

[68] Ibn Sa'd, *Tabaqat*, 2:119; Hakim, 4:519; *Shifa'*, 1:344; Bayhaqi, 2:66.

eaten the leaf, except the parts bearing the names of God." They went and found it to be so.[69]

- "A pestilence will break out during Jerusalem's conquest." This city was conquered during 'Umar's caliphate, and a widespread pestilence broke out and killed about 70,000 people in 3 days.[70]

God's Messenger predicted the establishment of Basra and Baghdad,[71] that treasures would pour into Baghdad from all over the world, and that the Arabs would fight the Turks and the people living around the Caspian Sea,[72] most of whom would later convert and rule the Arabs in their own lands. He said: "Non-Arabs will predominate among you, con-

---

[69] Ibn Kathir, *al-Bidaya*, 3:96; Bayhaqi, 2:311; *Shifa'*, 1:345; Ibn Hisham, 1:371.

[70] Bukhari, 7:168; Muslim, no. 2219; Ibn Hanbal, 4:195.

[71] Basra: *al-Jami' al-Saghir*, 6:268, related by Abu Dawud; Baghdad: *al-Bidaya wa al-Nihaya*, 10:102; also related by Abu Nu'aym and Khatib.

[72] *Al-Shifa'*, 1:337, related by Bukhari, Muslim, Abu Dawud, and Tirmidhi.

suming your booty and striking off your heads."[73]

- "Young, evil Qurayshis will ruin my community."[74] This foretold such wicked Umayyad leaders as Yazid and Walid. He also predicted that people in certain areas, such as Yamama, would apostasize,[75] and said during the Battle of Khandaq: "After this, neither the Quraysh nor the Confederates will fight me, but I will fight them."[76]

- The Prophet foretold his death a few months before it happened: "One of God's slaves has been given a choice and has chosen that which is with God."[77]

---

[73] *Majma' al-Zawa'id,* 7:310, related by Hakim, Tayalisi, and Ibn Hanbal.

[74] Bukhari, 9:60; Ibn Hanbal, 2:288; Hakim, *Mustadrak*, 4:479.

[75] Bukhari, 4:247; Muslim, 4:1781.

[76] Ibn Hanbal, 4:262, also related by Bukhari, Ibn Hibban, and Tabarani.

[77] Muslim, no. 2382; also related by Bukhari and Tirmidhi.

- "One of his (Zayd ibn Sawhan) limbs will precede him to Paradise."[78] This came true when Zayd lost a hand during a battle.

These predictions related to the Unseen constitute only one of his 10 kinds of miracles. We did not mention one of these kinds here, and summarized the other four kinds related to predictions in the Twenty-fifth Word. Anyone with an uncorrupted mind and heart can consider just this one kind together with the other four in order to believe that Muhammad is God's Messenger and was instructed by the All-Majestic One, the Creator of everything and the Knower of the Unseen.

SEVENTH SIGN: We mention a few examples of the Prophet's miracles related to increasing food that have the certainty of *tawatur* in meaning. But before continuing, some introductory comments are appropriate.

Each miracle related below was transmitted through various—sometimes as many as 16—channels. Most took place before large groups and were narrated by many persons of truth and good

---

[78] *Majma' al-Zawa'id*, 9:398, related by Bayhaqi, Ibn Adiyy, and Abu Ya'la.

repute. For example, one of the 70 people fed with four handfuls of food relates the incident while the rest remain silent (i.e., they do not contradict him). Their silence indicates agreement. This is especially true for the truthful, straightforward, and honest Companions who reject and oppose all falsehood. The incidents given below are narrated by many people and confirmed by the witnesses' silence, thus making each incident definite to the degree of *tawatur* in meaning.

Moreover, history books and biographies of the Prophet record that the Companions, next to preserving the Qur'an and its verses, did their best to record and preserve the Messenger's deeds and words, especially those concerning miracles and Divine Commands, and to confirm their authenticity. They never neglected even an apparently insignificant act or state of the Prophet, as confirmed by the books of Tradition.

While the Prophet was alive, the miracles and Traditions forming the basis of religious injunctions were written down by many Companions, especially the "Seven 'Abdullahs," notably 'Abdullah ibn 'Abbas (the "Interpreter of the Qur'an") and 'Abdullah ibn 'Amr ibn al-'As. Some 30 or 40 years later, thousands of Tabi'un researchers recorded these, and later on the four imams of Islamic jurisprudence and thousands of discerning Traditionists also would write them down and transmit them.

Two centuries after the Prophet's migration, the compilers of the six esteemed and most authentic books of Traditions, at the head of whom are Imam al-Bukhari and Imam Muslim, shouldered the task of preserving the Traditions. In the meantime, meticulous critics identified false reports produced by heretics or careless and ignorant people.

In later centuries, Traditions continued to be distinguished from fabrications and distortions by people of profound learning and such meticulous researchers as Ibn al-Jawzi and Jalal al-Din al-Suyuti, who was honored many times while awake with the presence and conversation of God's Messenger, as confirmed by those of spiritual realization.

Thus the miracles cited below come down to us through numerous safe and trustworthy hands, for which we thank God, since this is by His grace. No one has the right to doubt their authenticity. Examples of authentically narrated miracles concerning the Prophet's increasing of food through his blessing are as follows:

FIRST EXAMPLE: Sahih al-Bukhari, Sahih al-Muslim, and the other six most authentic books of Tradition, relate that during the feast celebrating the Prophet's marriage to Zaynab, Umm Sulaym (Anas' mother) fried a few handfuls of dates and asked Anas to take them to the Prophet. He did so, and was told: "Go and invite so-and-so (naming some people) and whoever else you meet."

Anas did as he was told, and gradually about 300 Companions filled the Prophet's room and the large hall where the poor, learned Companions lived. The Prophet told them: "Make circles of ten." Putting his hand on the dates, he supplicated and told the people to help themselves. Each person ate until satisfied. Then he asked Anas to clear the table. Anas later related: "I could not tell if there was more food when I set out the dish or when I removed it."[79]

SECOND EXAMPLE: Abu Ayyub al-Ansari, who hosted the Prophet for some months after his emi-

---

[79] Bukhari, 4:234; Bayhaqi, *Dala'il*, 3:465; also related by Muslim.

gration, relates: "I made a meal sufficient for two people: God's Messenger and Abu Bakr. The Prophet, however, told me to invite 30 distinguished Ansaris (Helpers). Thirty men came and ate. He then asked me to invite another 60, which I did. They also came and ate. God's Messenger then told me to invite 70 more, which I did. They came and ate. There was still food left in the bowl when they finished eating. After witnessing that miracle, all who had eaten took the oath of allegiance. One hundred and eighty men ate food prepared for two."[80]

THIRD EXAMPLE: 'Umar, Abu Hurayra, Salama al-Aqwa, and Abu 'Amrat al-Ansari report that during a military campaign the army had no food. The Messenger, upon being informed, told them to gather all of their food. Everyone brought a few dates—the largest amount was a few handfuls—and put them on a mat. Salama relates: "I estimated the amount to be the equivalent of a reclining goat." God's Messenger prayed for its increase and called everyone to bring his bowl. They rushed forward, and each soldier's bowl was filled. Even

---

[80] *Al-Shifa'*, 1:292; related by Tabarani, Ibn Kathir, and Bayhaqi.

then, some was food left over. One Companion who was there later said: "I realized from the way the dates became abundant that there would be enough even if all people on Earth came."[81]

FOURTH EXAMPLE: Authentic books of Tradition, including Bukhari and Muslim, report that 'Abd al-Rahman ibn Abu Bakr related: "We, 130 Companions, accompanied God's Messenger on an expedition. Dough from four handfuls of wheat was prepared to make bread, a goat was slaughtered and cooked, and its liver and kidneys were roasted. I swear by God that God's Messenger gave each of us a piece from the roasted parts and put the cooked meat in the bowls. We ate until we were full, and still there was some left over. I loaded it onto a camel."[82]

FIFTH EXAMPLE: As recorded in authentic books, Jabir al-Ansari relates under oath: "During the Battle of Ahzab or of Khandaq (the Trench), our food seemed to be undiminished even after about 1,000 men had eaten bread made from four handfuls of barley and (meat from) a young

---

[81] Muslim, no. 1729, also related by Bukhari.

[82] Muslim, no. 2057; Hakim, 2:618; also related by Bukhari and Ibn Hanbal.

cooked goat. The food was cooked in my house. And after everyone ate and left, the pot was still boiling with meat and bread was still being made from the dough. God's Messenger had put water from his mouth into the dough and into the pot, and then prayed for abundance."[83] Since this event was witnessed by 1,000 people, was related by Jabir with an oath, and no one is reported to have contradicted it, it can be considered as definite as if it were related by 1,000 people.

SIXTH EXAMPLE: As related in an authentic way, Abu Talha (Anas' uncle) said: "God's Messenger fed 70 to 80 people with a small amount of rye bread that Anas brought under his arm. The Messenger ordered the bread broken into small pieces and then prayed for abundance. Since there was not enough space for everyone, the people ate in shifts of ten. Everyone left satisfied."[84]

SEVENTH EXAMPLE: Authentic books of Tradition, including *Shifa' al-Sharif* and *Sahih al-Muslim*, report that Jabir al-Ansari said: "A man

---

[83] Muslim, no. 3029; Bukhari, 5:138; Ibn Hanbal, Musnad, 3:218.

[84] Bukhari, 4:234; Muslim, no. 2040; Bayhaqi, 6:88; Ibn Hanbal, 3:218.

asked God's Messenger for food to feed his family. The Messenger gave him half a load of barley. He and his household ate from it for a long time. When they noticed it was not decreasing, they measured it to see how much it had been reduced. This ended the blessing of abundance, and the barley began to dwindle. When the man told God's Messenger what had happened, he replied: 'If you had not measured it, it would have sufficed you for a lifetime.'"[85]

EIGHTH EXAMPLE: Such authentic books as *Sunan al-Tirmidhi, Sunan al-Nasa'i, Dala'il al-Bayhaqi, Shifa' al-Sharif,* and others quote Samura ibn Jundub as relating that a bowl of meat brought to God's Messenger fed groups of people from morning until evening.[86] As explained in the introduction on these Traditions' authenticity, it is as if everyone present related this event and that Samura related it on their behalf and with their approval.

NINTH EXAMPLE: As related by such reliable and trusted researchers as Qadi 'Iyad (author of

---

[85] *Shifa'*, 1:91; Muslim, no. 2281; Bayhaqi, 6:114.

[86] Tirmidhi, no. 2629; also related by Darimi, Hakim, and Ibn Hanbal.

Shifa' al-Sharif), Ibn Abi Shayba, and Tabarani, Abu Hurayra says: "God's Messenger told me to invite poor people of the Suffa[87] who used the mosque's hall as their home. There were more than 100 of them, and I searched for and summoned them all. One plate of food was put before us. We all ate from it as much as we wished. When we rose, the plate was as full as it had been when placed before us. However, our finger marks on the food showed that we had eaten from it."[88] Although only Abu Hurayra narrates this event, it is as definite as if each member of the Suffa had narrated it, since Abu Hurayra narrates in their name and relies on their confirmation. Would such perfect, truthful people remain silent if the narration were not true?

TENTH EXAMPLE: Imam 'Ali narrates that God's Messenger gathered 'Abd al-Muttalib's descendants, about 40 people, some of whom

---

[87] The people of the Suffa were the poor Muhajirin (emigrants to Madina) who lived in the mosque's hall and devoted themselves to Islam, particularly to preserving Prophetic Traditions. The Messenger provided their livelihood. (Tr.)

[88] *Shifa'*, 1:293; Bayhaqi, 6:101; related by Tabarani and Ibn Hanbal.

could eat a young camel and drink more than a gallon of milk at one meal. But God's Messenger had prepared only a handful of food. They ate until satisfied, and the amount of food did not decrease. Then the Messenger brought them a wooden bowl of milk that might be enough for only three or four people. They drank until satisfied, and the amount of milk did not decrease.[89] This miracle is as definite as 'Ali's bravery and loyalty.

ELEVENTH EXAMPLE: At the wedding feast of 'Ali and Fatima, God's Messenger told Bilal: "Have some bread made from a few handfuls of flour, and have a young camel be slaughtered." Bilal narrates: "I brought the food, and he put his hand over it for a blessing. Later, the Companions came in groups, ate, and left. The Messenger prayed for the abundance of the remaining food and sent a full bowl to each of his wives, saying that they should eat and feed whoever came to them."[90] Such blessed abundance was necessary for such a blessed marriage.

---

[89] *Majma' al-Zawa'id*, 8:302, related by Ibn Hanbal, Bazzar, and Tabarani.

[90] *Shifa'*: 1:297; Bayhaqi, *Dala'il,* 3:160.

TWELFTH EXAMPLE: Imam Ja'far al-Sadiq related that Fatima cooked enough food only for herself and 'Ali. She sent 'Ali to invite God's Messenger to eat with them. He came and told them to send a dish of food to each of his wives and then put the remaining food aside for him, 'Ali, Fatima, and their children. Fatima says: "When we removed the pot, it was still full to the brim. By God's Will, we ate from it for quite a long time."[91] I wonder why you do not believe this miracle as if you yourself had seen it, for it reaches us through such an illustrious and respected line of narrators. Even Satan could not dispute it!

THIRTEENTH EXAMPLE: Such truthful Tradition authorities as Abu Dawud, Ahmad ibn Hanbal, and Bayhaqi narrate from Dukayn al-Ahmad ibn Sa'd al-Muzayn, from Nu'man ibn Muqarrin al-Ahmad al-Muzayn, who along with his six brothers was a Companion, and from Jarir the following incident originally reported by 'Umar and transmitted through various channels:

---

[91] *Shifa'*, 1:294; Ibn Hajar, *al-Matalib al-'Aliya*, 4:73. The chain of transmission is as follows: from his father Muhammad al-Baqir, from his father Imam Zayn al-'Abidin, from 'Ali.

"God's Messenger once told 'Umar: 'Provide food for 400 horsemen of the Ahmasi tribe for their journey.' 'Umar responded: 'O Messenger of God, all the provisions put together are about the size of a young camel sitting down.' The Prophet told him to give it to them. From half a load of dates, 'Umar gave them an amount that satisfied 400 horsemen. He would later say when reporting this event: 'The food did not decrease.'"[92] This is confirmed by the witnesses' silence. Do not ignore such narrations just because they are related by only two or three people, for confirmation by silence gives their meaning the authority and certainty of *tawatur* by meaning.

FOURTEENTH EXAMPLE: As narrated by authentic books of Tradition, including *Bukhari* and *Muslim*, Jabir's father died while deep in debt to Jews. Jabir gave all of his father's possessions to the creditors, but they were not satisfied. The fruits in his orchard would not pay off the remaining debts for years. God's Messenger said: "Pick the fruits and heap them up." He did so. The

---

[92] *Majma' al-Zawa'id*, 8:304; Bayhaqi, 5:365; Ibn Hanbal, 5:445.

Messenger then walked around them and prayed. After Jabir had paid his father's debt, fruit equal to the orchard's annual yield still remained.

According to another narration, what remained was equal to what he had given the creditors. This greatly astounded the Jewish creditors.[93] Since this miracle is related on behalf of its witnesses, its meaning has the assurance of *tawatur*.

FIFTEENTH EXAMPLE: Such meticulous researchers as Tirmidhi and Bayhaqi quote Abu Hurayra as saying: "During a battle ("During the Battle of Tabuk" according to another narration) the army ran out of food. God's Messenger asked: 'Isn't there anything at all?' I replied: 'I have a few ("15" in another version) dates left in my saddle bag.' He told me to bring them, which I did. Putting his hand in the bag, he took out a handful of dates and prayed for abundance while putting them on a plate. Then he called the army in groups of ten. After everyone had eaten, God's Messenger, said to me: 'Take that (bag) which you brought, hold on to it, and do not turn it upside

---

[93] Bukhari, 3: 210; Abu Dawud, 1:17; also related by Ibn Hanbal and Nasa'i.

down.' I took the bag, put my hand into it, and found therein as many dates as I had brought. Later, during the time of the Prophet and then of Abu Bakr, 'Umar, and 'Uthman, I ate from those dates."[94]

Abu Hurayra was a constant and important student and disciple at the Suffa, the sacred school of God's Messenger, the teacher of the universe and the pride of creation. Moreover, the Prophet had prayed for Abu Hurayra to have a strong memory. Thus this miracle, which took place before many people, must be regarded as definitive as if it had been related by the whole army.

SIXTEENTH EXAMPLE: Accurate books of Tradition, *Bukhari* included, relate that Abu Hurayra was once hungry and followed God's Messenger into his home. Seeing a bowl of milk that had been brought as a gift, God's Messenger told him to invite the people of the Suffa. Abu Hurayra relates: "I said to myself: 'I could drink all of this milk, as I am most in need of it.' But

---

[94] In another version, Abu Hurayra said: "I gave many loads of them in the way of God. When 'Uthman was martyred, the dates and the bag were plundered." *Shifa'*, 1:295, related by Ibn Hanbal, Bayhaqi, and Tirmidhi.

since it was the Prophet's order, I fetched them all—more than 100 people. The Messenger told me to offer the milk to them. I gave the bowl to each, one by one, and each of them drank until satisfied. Finally the Prophet told me: 'We two have been left. You drink first!' As I was drinking, he repeatedly said to me: 'Drink more,' until I said: 'I swear by the Majestic One Who sent you with the truth that I am too full to drink any more.' Then the Prophet drank the rest, saying: 'In the Name of God' and praising Him.'"[95]

This miracle, as pure and sweet as milk itself, is related in all six authentic books of Tradition, above all by Imam Bukhari, who memorized 500,000 Traditions. In addition, it is narrated by Abu Hurayra, a loyal, celebrated student of the Prophet's sacred school of the Suffa and a Companion with a keen memory. He represented all other students of that school, and so his report has the certainty of *tawatur*.

How could such a truthful person, who devoted his life to Islam and the Prophetic Traditions, who heard and related the Tradition that: "Whoever tells

---

[95] Tirmidhi, no. 2479; Bukhari, 8:120; Hakim, 3:15; Bayhaqi, 4:101.

a lie concerning me on purpose should prepare for his seat in the Fire," relate an unfounded incident or saying? Doing so would harm the value and authenticity of all the Traditions he had memorized and make him a target of contradiction by the people of the Suffa!

> O Lord, for the sake of the blessing You have bestowed on Your Messenger, bestow abundance on the favors You have provided for us!

An important point: Weak things become strong when joined together. Fine twisted threads become a strong rope and, when wound, strong ropes cannot be broken. Now, from 15 kinds of miracles we have shown only one kind, which deals with the blessing of abundance. The 16 examples cited so far constitute only one part of this kind. Each example is strong enough to prove Prophethood. If, however—supposing the impossible—some were regarded as weak, still we could not properly call them such, for whatever is united with the strong also becomes strong.

When considered together, the 16 examples mentioned above indicate a great and strong miracle with the definitive strength of *tawatur* in meaning. And this miracle, when joined with the

14 other parts of the miracles of abundance not yet cited, manifests a supreme miracle as strong as the most unbreakable cable. Finally, add this supreme miracle to the other 14 kinds of miracles and see what a definite, decisive, and irrefutable proof they provide for Muhammad's Prophethood.

Thus the pillar of his Prophethood, formed by such a collection of proofs, is as strong as a mountain. You may understand the doubts of those who do not believe in his Prophethood as the doubts of those who regard the sublime and established heavens as feeble or fragile because they do not have visible pillars. These miracles of abundance illustrate that the Prophet was such a beloved envoy and honored servant of the All-Compassionate and All-Generous One that He, Who supplies the provisions of creation, changed His usual way of acting whenever necessary and sent him banquets from the Unseen—as He creates from nothingness.

Arabia suffers scarcities of water and agriculture. And so its people, especially the Companions in the earliest period of Islam, were exposed to frequent food and water shortages. As a result, some of his greatest miracles were connected with food and water.

Rather than proving Prophethood, these wonders were responses to need, a Divine gift, a favor of the Lord, and a banquet provided by the Most Merciful One for those who confirmed his Prophethood before witnessing any miracles. When the miracles occurred, their belief and conviction became even stronger, brighter, and more vivid.

EIGHTH SIGN: This section concerns miracles connected with water.

INTRODUCTION: If the report of an incident involving many people is not contradicted, the incident definitely occurred, even if reported by only one or two individuals, for people, by their very nature, are inclined to call a lie a lie. If the people in question were Companions, who were more intolerant of lies than ordinary people, if the incidents narrated concerned God's Messenger, and if the individual narrator was a well-known Companion, then that narrator narrates on behalf of all witnesses.

In any case, each miracle cited below came down through various lines of transmission and was entrusted by many Companions to thousands of exacting Tabi'un scholars. These scholars, in turn, transmitted them to the authorities of the next age. Each age's meticulous researchers passed them on to their successors with the utmost care and respect. Thus they reached us after passing through thousands of reliable hands.

Besides, the texts of the Traditions complied while the Prophet and his Rightly-Guided Caliphs were still alive safely reached the hands of the most brilliant Tradition scholars, such as Bukhari and Muslim, who, through the most careful examination and classification, collected, presented, and taught them. May God reward them abundantly!

The flowing of water from the fingers of God's Messenger, as well as many people's drinking from it, has the certainty of *tawatur*, for it is related by those who are incapable of agreeing upon a lie. In addition, this occurred three times before large groups of people. Many discerning researchers (especially Bukhari, Muslim, Imam Malik, Imam Shu'ayb, and Imam Qatada) transmit this miracle from a group of renowned Companions (among them Anas, Jabir, and Ibn Mas'ud). Out of numerous examples of such miracles, we mention only nine here.

FIRST EXAMPLE: Bukhari, Muslim, and other authentic books of Tradition relate from Anas that: "There were 300 of us with God's Messenger at Zawra. He told us to perform *wudu'* (ablution) for the afternoon prayer, but we could not find enough water. He ordered us to bring a little water, which we did, and he dipped his hands into it. I saw water run from his fingers like a fountain. All 300 people performed *wudu'* with that water and drank from it."[96] Anas relates this incident on behalf of 300 persons. Would they have remained silent if he were lying?

SECOND EXAMPLE: Reliable books of Tradition, particularly *Sahih al-Bukhari* and *Sahih al-Muslim*, report Jabir ibn 'Abdullah al-Ansari as saying: "We (1,500 people) got thirsty during the expedition of Hudaybiya. God's Messenger performed *wudu'* from a leather water-bag (*qirba*) and then dipped his hand into it. I saw water flow from his fingers like a fountain. All 1,500 people drank from it and filled their water-bags." Salim ibn Abi al-Ja'd later asked Jabir how many people had been there, and the latter replied: "The

---

[96] Nasa'i, 1:60; Bukhari, 4:233; Muslim, No. 2279; Tirmidhi, No. 3635.

water would have been enough for even 100,000 people, but there were only 1,500 of us."[97]

Since this miracle was witnessed by 1,500 people, the number of its reporters should be regarded as 1,500, because people tend to resist and refuse lies. As for the Companions, who sacrificed their souls and possessions, fathers and mothers, tribes and homeland for the sake of truth and veracity, could they have remained silent if confronted with a lie, especially after hearing the Prophet's warning: "Whoever tells a lie concerning me on purpose should prepare for his seat in the Fire."? Their silence indicates acceptance.

THIRD EXAMPLE: According to the authentic books of Tradition, above all al-Bukhari and al-Muslim, Jabir relates: "During the campaign of Buwat, God's Messenger ordered ablution. We replied that there was no water. The Messenger told us to try and find just a little. We fetched a small amount of water. He placed his hand over it and recited a prayer, which I could not hear, and then asked for the largest water trough in the caravan. They brought it to me, and I placed it before

---

[97] Muslim, no. 1856; Bukhari, 4:234; Bayhaqi, 4:110.

God's Messenger. He placed his hands in it, with his fingers apart, while I poured that little water onto his hands. I saw water run abundantly from his fingers and fill the trough. I called those who needed water. After they drank and took water for *wudu'*, I told the Prophet that everybody had come. He lifted his hands, leaving the trough still full to the brim."[98]

This miracle has the certainty of *tawatur* in meaning, because Jabir, at that time the Prophet's servant and thus having first place in the incident, relates it in the name of all witnesses. Ibn Mas'ud, who also reported it, says: "I saw the water flow like a fountain from the Prophet's fingers."[99]

Consider these three examples together and see what an irrefutable and definite miracle this is. Joined together, they prove that water flowing from the Prophet's fingers is explicit *tawatur*. This miracle is so great that even Moses' miracle of causing water to run from 12 different points of a rock cannot be considered its equivalent. Water gushing from a rock is possible, and examples can

---

[98] Muslim, no. 3006-14.

[99] Bukhari, 4:235, also related by Tirmidhi and Nasa'i.

be found among ordinary events, but there is no parallel for water flowing abundantly from flesh and bone.

FOURTH EXAMPLE: Imam Malik narrates in his *Muwatta'* from Mu'adh ibn Jabal that: "During the expedition of Tabuk, we came across a fountain that was hardly flowing—the jet was about as thick as a thin string. God's Messenger told us to collect a small amount of its water. Some brought a little in their palms, with which God's Messenger washed his face and hands. Then we put it back in the fountain. Suddenly the stream supplying the fountain's water cleared, and water began to flow so profusely that there was enough for the whole army."

Imam Ibn Ishaq, one of the narrators, reports: "The fountain's well rushed underground with a noise like thunder. God's Messenger told Mu'adh that he might live long enough to see this place change into gardens." And so it happened.[100]

FIFTH EXAMPLE: Bukhari (from Bara') and (from Salama ibn al-Akwa'), as well as other accurate books (from other narrators), relate:

---

[100] *Muwatta'*, Safar, 2; Ibn Hanbal, 5:228; also related by Bukhari and Muslim.

"Four hundred of us came across a well during the expedition of Hudaybiya. There was hardly enough water for 50 people. We drew all the water out of the well. God's Messenger came and sat beside the well and asked for a bucketful of water, which we fetched. He put some of his saliva into the bucket, prayed, and then poured this water back into the well. Suddenly the water began to gush and rose to the well's brim. The whole army and their animals drank from it until they were satisfied, and then filled their water bags."[101]

SIXTH EXAMPLE: Authentic Tradition books, such those of Muslim and Ibn Jarir al-Tabari particularly, relate through Abu Qatada: "We were going for help, as the commanders had been martyred in the Battle of Mu'ta. I had a water bag with me. God's Messenger had told me: 'Keep your water bag carefully, for it will be of great use to us.' Soon after that, thirst seized us. We were 72 (300 according to al-Tabari). God's Messenger told me: 'Bring your water bag.' I did so. He took it and brought its brim to his lips. I do not know whether he breathed into it or not. Then all 72 of

---

[101] Bukhari, 4:234; Bayhaqi, 4:110; also related by Muslim.

us drank from it and filled our water bags. When I took it back, it was still as full as it had been before."[102]

Reflect on this miracle and say: "O God, bestow upon him and his household peace and blessings as many as there are drops of water."

SEVENTH EXAMPLE: Authentic books of Tradition, in particular *Sahih al-Bukhari* and *Sahih al-Muslim*, report that 'Imran ibn Husayn said: "Our water ran out on a military campaign. The Messenger told me and 'Ali: 'A woman in such-and-such a place is making her way with her beast, which is laden with water bags. Go and bring her.' 'Ali and I found her with her load exactly as and where described, and brought her (to him). He ordered: 'Pour some water into a vessel.' We did so. After he prayed for abundance, we put the water back into its bag. Then the Messenger said: 'Let everyone come and fill his bag.' Everyone came, drank, and filled their bags. Afterwards, he said that something should be collected for the woman, so they filled her skirt with what they collected."

---

[102] Muslim, no. 681; Abu Dawud, no. 437-41; Abu Nu'aym, 4:282.

'Imran adds: "I imagined that the two water bags were filling unceasingly. God's Messenger told her: 'You can go now. We took none of your water; rather, God gave us water (from His treasure).'"[103]

EIGHTH EXAMPLE: Some Traditionists, primarily Ibn Khuzayma in his *Sahih*, report that 'Umar said: "We ran out of water during the campaign of Tabuk. Some of us had to slaughter our camels and drink what was inside. Abu Bakr appealed to God's Messenger to pray for rain. He raised his hands to pray, and had hardly lowered them when clouds gathered and a heavy rain began to fall. After we filled our vessels, the clouds withdrew. This rain was restricted to our area, for it did not go beyond where we were located."[104] Thus chance had nothing to do with this incident; it was wholly a miracle of Prophet Muhammad.

NINTH EXAMPLE: 'Amr ibn Shu'ayb, the grandson of 'Abdullah ibn 'Amr ibn al-'As and whose narrations the four Imams trusted, relates that

---

[103] Muslim, 682; Bukhari, 4:233.

[104] *Majma' al-Zawa'id*, 6:194, related by Bazzar, Bayhaqi, and Tabarani.

before his Prophethood, God's Messenger traveled on a camel to Dhu al-Hijaz (near 'Arafat) with his uncle Abu Talib. When Abu Talib said he was thirsty, God's Messenger dismounted and stamped the ground. Water welled out, and Abu Talib drank from it.[105]

One discerning scholar states that although this is considered as *irhasat*, because it happened before his Prophethood was proclaimed,[106] it also can be regarded as a wonder of his Prophethood, because this water flowed in the same location for 1,000 years thereafter.

Similarly, 90 different narrations (but not 90 separate incidents) report miracles connected with water. The first seven examples are as definitely established in meaning as *tawatur*. Although the last two are not narrated through as many strong chains of transmission, authentic sources, primarily Imam Bayhaqi and Hakim,

---

[105] *Shifa'*, 1:290, Bayhaqi, 2:15; also related by Ibn Sa'd and Tabarani.

[106] *Irhasat*: The series of extraordinary incidents that happened before Prophet Muhammad's birth, at his birth, and before he declared his Prophethood. (Tr.)

report another miracle to support and confirm the one mentioned in the eighth example: 'Umar narrated that he appealed to God's Messenger to pray for rain, as the army needed water. God's Messenger raised his hands, clouds gathered at once, and enough rain fell to meet the army's need. After this, the clouds went away.[107] It was as if the clouds were sent to deliver water, for they came, dispensed enough water, and then disappeared.

Just as this narration supports the eighth example, Ibn al-Jawziya, too meticulous a researcher to reject many authentic Traditions as false, says: "This event took place during the Battle of Badr and is mentioned in: *And He sent down on you water from heaven to purify you thereby...* (8:11)." Since this verse refers to the event, its truth cannot be doubted. Besides, it is a frequently repeated and unanimously reported miracle that rain fell immediately after the Prophet raised his hands to pray. There were times, it is reported through *tawatur*, that when he raised his hands in the pulpit, rain would begin to fall before he lowered them.

---

[107] Abu Nu'aym, 2:523; also related by Hakim and Bayhaqi.

NINTH SIGN: One kind of miracle of God's Messenger is that trees obeyed his orders and approached him. This miracle, like those connected with water flowing from his fingers, has the certainty of *tawatur* in meaning. Many examples have been reported through various channels.

Trees uprooting themselves upon the Messenger's command and drawing near him can be considered explicit *tawatur*, because the best-known, trustworthy Companions (e.g., 'Ali, Ibn 'Abbas, Ibn Mas'ud, Ibn 'Umar, Ya'la ibn Murra, Jabir, Anas ibn Malik, Burayda, Usama ibn Zayd, and Ghaylan ibn Salama) reported the same miracle with certainty. Hundreds of Tabi'un scholars received their reports directly, which have come down to us and thus have the authority of multiple *tawatur*. This miracle therefore has the certainty of *tawatur* in meaning. We mention only a few examples.

FIRST EXAMPLE: Ibn Maja, Darimi, and Bayhaqi (through 'Ali and Anas ibn Malik), and Bazzar and Imam Bayhaqi (from 'Umar) report: "Three Companions narrated that God's Messenger was disturbed by the unbelievers' denial. He prayed: 'O Lord, show me a sign so that I will no longer heed anyone who contradicts me.' Anas relates that Gabriel also was present, and that upon his instruction God's Messenger called to a tree located at one side of the valley in which they were located. It left its place and drew near to him. He told it to go back, and so it returned and settled down in its place."[108]

SECOND EXAMPLE: Qadi 'Iyad, scholar of the Muslim West (North Africa and al-Andalus), relates in his *al-Shifa' al-Sharif* from 'Abdullah ibn 'Umar through a sound chain of the most eminent narrators: "A Bedouin approached God's Messenger during an expedition. The Messenger asked: 'Where are you going?' He replied: 'To my family.' The Messenger asked: 'Don't you desire something better?' When the Bedouin asked what that might be, God's Messenger replied: 'To bear witness that there is no god but God, alone with no partner, and that Muhammad is His servant and Messenger.' The Bedouin asked: 'Can you prove this?' God's Messenger replied: 'That tree at the side of the valley will bear witness.'"

---

[108] *Shifa'*, 1:302; related by Bayhaqi, Ibn Maja, Darimi, Bazzar, and Ibn Hanbal.

Ibn 'Umar relates the rest of the event: "That tree swayed, uprooted itself, left the soil, and drew near to God's Messenger. He asked it three times to testify, and each time it testified to his truthfulness. Then he ordered the tree to go back and settle down in its place, and it did so."[109]

Ibn Sahib al-Aslami relates that Burayda said: "Once a Bedouin asked for a miracle while we were with God's Messenger on an expedition. The Messenger pointed to a tree and told him: 'Tell that tree that God's Messenger summons it.' The tree swayed, freed itself, and drew near to the Messenger, saying: 'Peace be upon you, O Messenger of God!' The Bedouin said: 'Now tell it to return to its place.' When God's Messenger ordered it to do so, the tree went back. When the Bedouin said: 'Let me prostrate myself before you,' the Messenger answered: 'No one is allowed to do that.' The Bedouin said: 'Then I will kiss your hand,' and he allowed him to do so."[110]

THIRD EXAMPLE: Authentic books of Tradition, including Muslim's *Sahih*, quote Jabir as relating:

---

[109] *Shifa'*, 1:298; related by Tirmidhi, Ibn Hibban, Bayhaqi, and Hakim.

[110] *Shifa'*, 1:299; Bazzar, *Musnad*, 3:49.

"We accompanied God's Messenger on an expedition. He searched for a place to relieve himself. When he saw that there was no screened place, he went to two trees and pulled one of them by a branch next to the other one. The tree was like an obedient camel being pulled by its reins. He addressed them: 'Join together over me, by God's leave.' The trees did so and formed a screen. After relieving himself, he ordered them to go back to their places."[111] In another version, Jabir relates it with a very slight, insignificant difference.[112]

FOURTH EXAMPLE: Usama ibn Zayd, a brave commander and servant of God's Messenger, reports: "We accompanied God's Messenger on an expedition. Unable to find a screened place to relieve himself, he asked me: 'Do you see any trees or rocks?' When I said that I did, he told me: 'Go and say to the trees that God's Messenger orders them to join together so that he may relieve himself, and then tell the rocks to do the same.' I went and told them to do this, and I swear by God the trees joined together and the rocks formed a wall. After relieving himself, God's Messenger

---

[111] Muslim, no. 3006-12; Bayhaqi, 6:8.

[112] *Shifa'*, 1:299.

told me: 'Tell them to separate.' I swear by the Majestic One, in Whose hand is my soul, that the trees and rocks separated and went back to their places."[113]

These two incidents also were reported by Ya'la ibn Murra, Ghaylan ibn Salama al-Thaqafi, and Ibn Mas'ud in connection with the Battle of Hunayn.

FIFTH EXAMPLE: Imam Ibn Fawrak, known as the second Shafi'i on account of his excellence in jurisprudence and perfect character, reports: "God's Messenger sometimes felt sleepy while traveling on horseback. One night during the Battle of Ta'if, a lotus tree appeared in front of him. To make way for him and avoid harming his horse, the tree split in half and God's Messenger passed through it while riding his horse. That tree has remained so up to our time."[114]

SIXTH EXAMPLE: Ya'la reports: "During an expedition a *talha* or *samura* tree came and walked around God's Messenger, as if circumam-

---

[113] Ibid., 1:300, related by Bayhaqi, Ibn Hanbal, and Abu Ya'la.

[114] Ibid., 1:301.

bulating, and then went back to its place. God's Messenger said: 'It asked for God's permission to salute me.'"[115]

SEVENTH EXAMPLE: Traditionists quote Ibn Mas'ud as saying: "When the jinn of Nusaybin came to Batn al-Nakhl to be converted to Islam by God's Messenger, a tree informed him of their coming." Imam Mujahid relates from Ibn Mas'ud that when the jinn asked for a proof of his Prophethood, a tree came to the Messenger and then returned to its place on his order. This miracle was enough to convert them.[116]

Those who have heard of 1,000 similar miracles and still do not believe are even further astray than devils. Jinn describe such people as *the foolish ones among us [who used to] utter extravagant lies against God* (72:4).

EIGHTH EXAMPLE: Tirmidhi reports from Ibn 'Abbas: "God's Messenger asked a Bedouin: 'If that tree branch comes to me when I call it, will

---

[115] Shifa', 1:301; Hakim, 2:617; Ibn Hanbal, 4:170; Bayhaqi, 6:23.

[116] Bukhari, 5:58; also related by Muslim, Abu Dawud, Tirmidhi, and Ibn Hanbal.

you bear witness that I am the Messenger?' He replied that he would, and so the Messenger called to it. The branch broke off and jumped over near to him. It then jumped back to its place when the Messenger commanded it to do so."[117]

Many similar examples are reported through various narrations. Seven or eight ropes form a strong cable when they come together. In the same way, when these tree-related miracles reported by the most renowned Companions are taken together, they must have the certainty of *tawatur* in meaning or even in actual wording. In fact, they gain the degree of explicit *tawatur* through the Companions passing them down to the following generation.

In particular, such authentic books of Tradition as Bukhari's *Sahih*, Muslim's *Sahih*, Ibn Hibban's *Sahih*, and Tirmidhi's *Sunan* note and record the chain of transmitters (leading back to the Prophet's time) so soundly and convincingly that reading an account in Bukhari's *Sahih*, for instance, is equivalent to hearing it from the Companions.

When trees recognize God Almighty's Mes-

---

[117] Tirmidhi, no. 3632; Hakim, 2:620; Bayhaqi, 6:15.

senger, confirm his Messengership, call upon and salute him, and obey his orders, how can those unbelievers who call themselves human beings be considered anything but worthless pieces of wood and worthy of hellfire?

TENTH SIGN: This concerns the grieving pole, which is reported in the form of *tawatur* and reinforces the tree-related miracles. This event, which happened in the Prophet's Mosque before a vast congregation, consolidates and confirms such miracles, for the pole came from a tree. But this miracle itself is *mutawatir* (has the certainty of explicit *tawatur*), while miracles concerning trees are *mutawatir* when considered as a whole.

The Prophet used to lean on a date-palm pole while delivering a sermon in his mosque. However, when he began to deliver his sermons on the newly constructed pulpit, the congregation heard the pole moan like a camel. Its moaning ended only after the Messenger consoled it by putting his hand on it.

This miracle is widely known and has the certainty of explicit *tawatur*. It was reported through 15 different channels by an illustrious group of Companions, among them such eminent scholars and leading Tradition narrators as Anas ibn Malik and Jabir ibn 'Abdullah al-Ansari (both of whom served the Prophet), 'Abdullah ibn 'Umar, 'Abdullah ibn 'Abbas, Sahl ibn Sa'd, Abu Sa'id al-Khudri, Ubay ibn Ka'b, Burayda, and Umm Salama (mother of the believers). Hundreds of Tabi'un authorities received it from the Companions, and authentic books of Tradition, above all *Bukhari* and *Muslim*, transmitted it to the following centuries.

Jabir reports that God's Messenger used to lean against the pole, called the "date-palm trunk," when delivering a sermon in his mosque. After a pulpit was built, the Prophet would deliver his sermon from it. Due to this separation, the pole moaned like a pregnant camel. Anas relates that it moaned like a water buffalo and caused the mosque to tremble. Sahl ibn Sa'd says: "When it moaned, many people burst into tears."

According to Ubay ibn Ka'b, the pole sobbed so much that it split. Another report relates that God's Messenger said: "It moaned because it was separated from the recitation of God's Names (during the sermon)." According to another version, he said: "If I had not embraced and consoled it, it would have wept until the Day of Judgment because of its separation from the Messenger."

According to Burayda, the Messenger put his hand on the pole when it began to weep and said: "If you wish, I will restore you in the wood from whence you came so that you may be rooted again, perfectly flourishing, and yield fruit again. Or, if you wish, I will plant you in Paradise and God's friends will eat from your fruits." Then he listened to it, and the people in the mosque heard the pole say: "Plant me in Paradise, and God's friends will eat from my fruits in the place where there is no decay." God's Messenger replied that he would and added: "It has preferred the World of Eternity to the transitory one."

The well-known scholar Hasan al-Basri would weep whenever he recounted this miraculous event to his disciples, and would say: "A piece of wood demonstrates such love and ardor for God's noble, most beloved Messenger. You need to feel this love much more than a piece wood does."[118] And we say: "That is true, and love and ardor for

---

[118] Bukhari, *Sahih*, 4:237; Ibn Hanbal, *Musnad*, nos. 2236, 2237, 2400, 2401, 2430-32; Muslim, *Sahih*, no. 2374; Qadi 'Iyad, *al-Shifa' al-Sharif*, 1:304-5; Nasa'i, *Sunan*, 3:102;

him are possible by adhering to his illustrious Sunna and Shari'a."

QUESTION: Why were miracles of abundance concerning food and water not reported through as many channels as the grieving pole, even though more people saw them?

ANSWER: There are two kinds of miracles. Some affirmed his Prophethood. The grieving pole is of this kind, for it is a proof that strengthens the believers' belief, urges hypocrites to belief and sincerity, and causes unbelievers to believe. This is why everyone witnessed it and so much effort was exerted to spread it. The other kind of miracles involving food and water are wonders or Divine gifts, even banquets provided by the All-Merciful One because of need, rather than manifest miracles.

Although they are miraculous proofs of his Prophethood, their real significance is that God, Who creates hundreds of tons of dates from a single date-stone, provides a banquet for 1,000 people out of a little food and satiates a thirsty army

---

Tirmidhi, *Sunan*, No. 3631; Bayhaqi, *Dala'il al-Nubuwwa*, 6:66; Abu Nu'aym, *Dala'il al-Nubuwwa*, 2:399; Darimi, *Sunan*, No. 39; *Kanz al-'Ummal*, 12:411-18.

of holy warriors with water flowing abundantly from the Prophet's fingers. This is why each miracle related to food and water does not reach the degree of the miracle of the grieving pole.

However, examples of these two kinds of miracles are considered, in their entirety, to have been as widely reported as the grieving pole. Besides, while each person present could see only the effects (and not the incidents) of the abundant food and water, with some only witnessing their happening, the pole's moaning was heard by everyone. This is another reason why the latter was spread so widely.

QUESTION: The Companions preserved the record of the Prophet's every act and condition with the utmost care. So why are such important miracles not related through more than 10 or 12 lines of transmission? And why are the main reporters only Companions like Jabir, Anas, and Abu Hurayra, and not, for example, Abu Bakr and 'Umar?

ANSWER: The answer to the first part is given in the Fourth Sign's "Third Essential." Concerning the second part, just as a patient goes to a doctor, engineers are consulted about engineering matters, and muftis are asked about religious issues, some scholarly Companions were entrusted with and devoted themselves to instructing the following generations in the Prophetic Traditions. For example, Abu Hurayra devoted his life to preserving Traditions, while 'Umar shouldered administrative matters and the caliphate's problems. Thus 'Umar narrated only a few Traditions, for he had confidence in such people as Abu Hurayra, Anas, and Jabir to instruct the Muslims in the Traditions.

In fact, a Tradition can be considered as established if it is reported by a well-known person belonging to the truthful, sincere, and trusted Companions. Given this, there is no need for it to be related by others. This is why some significant incidents have only one, two, or three channels.

ELEVENTH SIGN: Here, we will cite only eight of countless examples of miracles concerning such inanimate objects as rocks and mountains.

FIRST EXAMPLE: Qadi 'Iyad reports, in his *Shifa' al-Sharif* and through an exalted chain of narrators from such great Tradition authorities as Bukhari, that Ibn Mas'ud, the Prophet's servant, says: "We could hear food glorifying God while eating with God's Messenger."[119]

SECOND EXAMPLE: Accurate books of Tradition report from Abu Dharr and Anas that Anas said: "We were with God's Messenger. He put some pebbles in his hand, and they began to glorify God. Then he placed them in Abu Bakr's hand, and they continued their glorification."[120]

Abu Dharr reports that God's Messenger then put the pebbles in the hands of 'Umar and 'Uthman, successively, and they continued their glorification. Both Anas and Abu Dharr add that God's Messenger finally put the pebbles in their hands, after which the pebbles stopped their glorification.[121]

THIRD EXAMPLE: 'Ali, Jabir, and 'A'isha narrate that rocks and mountains would say: "Peace be upon you, O Messenger of God," to God's Messenger. 'Ali says: "Whenever we walked in Makka's suburbs during the early part of his Prophethood, the trees and rocks we passed

---

[119] Bukhari, 4:235, Tirmidhi, no. 3712.

[120] *Shifa'*, 1:306; Bayhaqi, *Dala'il*, 6:66.

[121] *Shifa'*, 1:306; *Majma' al-Zawa'id*, 5:179; related by Tabarani and Bazzar.

would say: 'Peace be upon you, O Messenger of God.'"[122]

Jabir relates: "When God's Messenger came across a rock or a tree, they would say in submission to him: "Peace be upon you, O Messenger of God."[123] According to Jabir ibn Samura, God's Messenger once said: "I recognize a rock that used to greet me."[124] According to some, he was referring to the Ka'ba's Black Stone. 'A'isha narrated: "God's Messenger said: 'After Gabriel brought me the Message, every time I passed a rock or a tree it would say: "Peace be upon you, O Messenger of God."'"[125]

FOURTH EXAMPLE: 'Abbas relates that the Messenger of God covered 'Abbas and his four sons ('Abdullah, 'Ubaydullah, Fadl, and Qusam) with a piece of cloth and prayed: "O my Lord, this is my father's brother and these are his sons. Veil them from the Fire as I have veiled them with my robe." The house's roof, door, and walls

---

[122] Tirmidhi, no. 3630; Hakim, 2:607; Abu Nu'aym, 2:389.

[123] *Shifa'*, 1:307, related by Bayhaqi.

[124] Muslim, no. 2277; Tirmidhi, no. 3703; Ibn Hanbal, 5:89.

[125] *Shifa'*, 1:37; Bayhaqi, 2:135.

joined this prayer at once, saying: "Amen, Amen."[126]

FIFTH EXAMPLE: Imam Bukhari primarily, and such other Traditionists as Ibn Hibban, Abu Dawud, and Tirmidhi, report from Anas, Abu Hurayra, 'Uthman, and Sa'id ibn Zayd (two of those promised Paradise): "God's Messenger, Abu Bakr, 'Umar, and 'Uthman climbed Mount Uhud. The mountain, either in awe or because of joy, trembled. God's Messenger ordered it: 'Be still, O Uhud, for on you there is a Prophet, a truthful one, and two martyrs.'"[127] In this way, God's Messenger predicted the martyrdom of 'Umar and 'Uthman.

A supplement to this Tradition reports that God's Messenger, pursued by unbelievers during his migration to Madina, climbed Sabir mountain. The mountain said: "Please leave me, O Messenger of God, for I fear God will punish me if they strike you while you are on me." Upon this, Mount Thawr called to him: "Come to me, O Messenger of God!" This is why people of intu-

---

[126] *Majma' al-Zawa'id*, 9:269; Bayhaqi, 6:71; Ibn Maja, 2:209.

[127] Abu Dawud, no. 4651; Tirmidhi, no. 3781; also related by Bukhari, Muslim, Hakim, and Ibn Maja.

ition feel fear on Sabir and safety on Thawr.[128] This example indicates that these great mountains are God's servants who glorify Him and perform their duties. In addition, they know and love the Prophet.

Sixth example: 'Abdullah ibn 'Umar said: "While delivering a sermon on the pulpit, the Messenger of God recited: *They measure not God with His true measure. Earth altogether shall be His handful on the Day of Resurrection, and the heavens shall be rolled up in His right hand* (39:67), and added: 'God, the All-Compelling, glorifies Himself and says: "I am the All-Compelling, I am the All-Compelling, I am the Great and Exalted."' As he said this, the pulpit trembled so much that we feared God's Messenger would fall down."[129]

Seventh example: Ibn 'Abbas ("the scholar of the Ummah" and "the interpreter of the Qur'an") and Ibn Mas'ud (the Prophet's servant and a great Companion scholar) report that the Ka'ba con-

---

[128] *Shifa'*, 1:308; 'Ali al-Qari, *Sharh al-Shifa'*, 1:630.

[129] Muslim, 4:2147; Hakim, 2:252; related by Nasa'i and Ibn Hanbal.

tained 360 idols fixed to the stone with lead. On the day of Makka's conquest, God's Messenger pointed at them one by one with a curved stick, reciting: *Truth has come, and falsehood has vanished. Falsehood is ever certain to vanish* (17:81). Whichever idol he pointed at fell down. If he pointed to the idol's face, it fell backwards; if he pointed to the idol's back, it fell on its face. Thus they all fell down.[130]

EIGHTH EXAMPLE: This is the famous story of the monk Bahira. Before his Prophethood was proclaimed, God's Messenger traveled to Damascus with trading caravans belonging to his uncle Abu Talib and some other Qurayshi traders. They halted near the monastery where Bahira, a well-known recluse, was staying. He came out unexpectedly. When he saw Muhammad the Trustworthy among the caravan, he said: "He is the lord of the worlds and will be a Prophet." The Qurayshis asked: "How do you know this?" The holy monk answered: "I saw a piece of cloud over the caravan as you were coming. When you sat down, it moved toward his side and shadowed

---

[130] *Majma' al-Zawa'id*, 6:176, related by Bukhari, Muslim, and Tirmidhi.

him. I also noticed that rocks and trees seemed to prostrate before him. They do this only for Prophets."[131]

There are about 80 similar instances. Joined together, these eight examples form so strong an unbreakable chain. Considered as a whole, such miracles concerning inanimate objects bearing witness to Muhammad's Prophethood have the certainty of *tawatur* in meaning. Each instance derives additional strength from the others, just as a thin pillar is fortified by being joined to thick columns. Likewise, people on their own are weak. But when they join an army, each one has enough power to challenge 1,000 people.

TWELFTH SIGN: The next three examples, related to the eleventh sign, are very significant.

FIRST EXAMPLE: As established through all interpreters' meticulous verification and all Traditionists' reports, the verse: *When you threw, it was not you that threw, but God threw* (8:17), refers to the following incident: During the Battle of Badr, God's Messenger took a handful of soil

---

[131] Tirmidhi, no. 3699; Hakim, 2:615; Ibn Hisham, 1:115; *Shifa'*, 1:83.

and pebbles and threw them at the unbelievers' army, saying: "May your faces be deformed." The soil entered each unbeliever's eyes, and "May your faces be deformed" was heard by each one. They consequently became preoccupied with their eyes and had to retreat, although they had launched the attack.[132]

The Traditionists, most notably Imam Muslim, report that the same incident happened during the Battle of Hunayn. As a result, and by God's Power and permission, each one was hit in the face by a handful of soil and had to flee the battlefield, being preoccupied with their eyes.[133]

As these extraordinary events are beyond human capacity and material causes, the Qur'an declares: *When you threw, it was not you that threw, but God threw* (8:17).

SECOND EXAMPLE: Reliable Traditionists, above all Imam Bukhari and Imam Muslim, report that after the Battle of Khaybar a Jewess roasted, poisoned, and sent a goat to the Messenger. His Com-

---

[132] *Majma' al-Zawa'id*, 6:84; related by Abu Dawud, Ibn Hanbal, and Bayhaqi.

[133] Muslim, no. 1775.

panions had just begun to eat it when he suddenly said: "Withdraw your hands! It tells me that it is poisoned." Everyone stopped eating except Bishr ibn al-Bara', who had taken a morsel of it and later died because of the poison. God's Messenger sent for the Jewess (Zaynab). When asked why she had done it, she said: "I thought that if you were a Prophet it would not harm you, and that if you were a king it would save the people from you."[134]

Consider the following point, which adds to the miraculousness of this extraordinary event: According to one report, some Companions also heard the goat speaking. The Jews had tried to harm God's Messenger and his close Companions at the same time. However, the Prophet's warning proved true and their plot was unveiled and foiled. When the Prophet, whose Companions never heard an untrue statement from him, said: "This goat tells me that....," everyone believed him with the same certainty as if they had heard the goat themselves.

THIRD EXAMPLE: The following relates three

---

[134] Abu Dawud, *Muqaddima*, 11; Bukhari, 2:121; Hakim, 3:219; Darimi, 1:35; Ibn Hanbal, 1:305; Bayhaqi, 6:256.

instances of another miracle resembling those of Moses' whitened hand and staff.

First: Imam Ahmad ibn Hanbal relates on Abu Sa'id al-Khudri's authority and verifies that God's Messenger gave Qatada ibn Nu'man a stick on a dark rainy night, saying: "This stick will light your surroundings as far as 7 meters. When you get home, you will see a black shadow that is Satan. Drive him away from your home." Qatada left with the stick, which was emitting light like the Moses' whitened hand. When he arrived home, he found the person described and drove him away.[135]

Second: During the Battle of Badr, which was a source of wonders, Ukkasha ibn Mihsan al-Asad broke his sword while fighting the polytheists. God's Messenger replaced his broken sword with a stick and told him to continue fighting. Suddenly, by God's power and permission, the stick changed into a long white sword. He fought with it and kept it with him until he was martyred

---

[135] *Majma' al-Zawa'id*, 2:166, related by Ibn Hanbal, Ibn Khuzayma, and Hakim.

during the Battle of Yamama.[136] This incident is indisputable, for Ukkasha was so proud of that sword that throughout his life it was widely known as "the aid."

Third: Ibn 'Abd al-Barr, one of the most brilliant scholars of his time, relates and verifies that 'Abdullah ibn Jahsh, a cousin of God's Messenger, broke his sword during the Battle of Uhud. The Messenger gave him a stick, which then became a sword in his hand. Ibn Jahsh fought with it, and that miracle remained a sword after the battle.[137] Years later, as reported by Ibn Sayyid al-Nas in his biography of the Prophet, it was sold to Buqhai Turki for 200 dirhams.[138] These two swords are miracles like Moses' staff, except that they remained swords thereafter, while Moses' staff lost its miraculous aspect after his death.

THIRTEENTH SIGN: Another type of miracle, a *mutawatir* one with various examples, is the Prophet's healing of the sick and wounded with his breath. In their entirety, such miracles are

---

[136] *Sira ibn Hisham*, 1:637; Bayhaqi, 4:97; Ibn al-Jawzi, *Zad al-Ma'ad*, 3:186.

[137] *Isti'ab*, 3:879; Ibn Hajar, *al-Isaba*, no. 4583; also related by Bayhaqi.

[138] *'Uyun al-Athar*, 2:20; Ibn Hajar, *al-Isaba*, no. 4583.

mutawatir in meaning. Certain incidents also have the certainty of *tawatur* in meaning. The rest should be regarded as authentic according to the scientific principles of Tradition, although their narration depends on only one chain of transmission, because they are related and verified by discerning leaders of this science. Out of many relevant examples, we cite only a few:

FIRST EXAMPLE: Qadi 'Iyad reports in his *Shifa'*, through numerous channels and a chain of exalted narrators from Sa'd ibn Abi Waqqas, a servant and military commander of God's Messenger, commander-in-chief of the army that conquered Persia during 'Umar's caliphate, and one of the ten Companions promised Paradise during their life.

He said: "I was beside God's Messenger during the Battle of Uhud. He shot arrows at the unbelievers until his bow was broken, after which he began to give his arrows to me. Each time he gave me a featherless arrow, he ordered me to shoot it, which I did. And it flew like one with feathers, piercing an unbeliever's body. Meanwhile, Qatada ibn Nu'man was hit and one of his eyeballs protruded. God's Messenger used his hand to replace the eyeball in its socket. The eye healed at once, as if nothing had happened, and became better than the other one."[139]

This incident became so well-known that when one of Qatada's grandsons met Caliph 'Umar ibn 'Abd al-'Aziz, he presented himself with the following poetical statement:

> I am the son of the person
> whose eye protruded over his cheek,
> But was wonderfully restored
> by the hand of Mustafa;
> Then it became as it had been before;
> it was the most beautiful of eyes,
> and most wonderful was its restoration.

During the Battle of Yawm Dhiqarad, an arrow hit Abu Qatada's face. God's Messenger wiped the injured man's face, and Abu Qatada said: "I never felt the pain, nor did the wound fester."[140]

SECOND EXAMPLE: Authentic Tradition books, primarily *Sahih al-Bukhari* and *Sahih Muslim*, report: 'Ali, who was suffering greatly from sore eyes, was appointed standard-bearer during the Battle of Khaybar. The pain ceased when God's

---

[139] *Shifa'*, 1:322, related by Ibn Ishaq, Tabarani, and Bayhaqi.

[140] *Shifa'*, 1:322, related by Tirmidhi and Bayhaqi.

Messenger applied his healing saliva to 'Ali's eyes, and his eyes became much better. The next morning, 'Ali joined the battle and, pulling up the citadel's heavy iron gate and using it as a shield, conquered the stronghold of Khaybar.[141] In the same battle, Salama ibn Akwa's leg wound was healed when God's Messenger breathed upon it.[142]

THIRD EXAMPLE: The Prophet's biographers, including al-Nasa'i, relate that 'Uthman ibn Hunayf said: "Pray for my eyes to open." God's Messenger told him to perform ablution, pray two *rak'ats*, and say: "O God, my appeal is to You, and I turn toward You through Prophet Muhammad, the Prophet of mercy. O Muhammad, I turn toward God through you, that He uncover my sight. O God, make him my intercessor." He went to do as he was told. When he returned, we saw that his eyes had been opened already.[143]

FOURTH EXAMPLE: Ibn Wahb, a great Tradition

---

[141] Bukhari, 4:58; Ibn Hanbal, 1:85; also related by Muslim and Tabarani.

[142] Bukhari, 5:170; *Shifa'*, 1:323.

[143] *Al-Jami' al-Saghir*, no. 1290, related by Nasa'i, Tirmidhi, Ibn Maja, Ibn Khuzayma, and Hakim.

authority, reports: When Mu'awwidh ibn 'Afra, one of the 14 martyrs of the Battle of Badr, fought with Abu Jahl, the accursed Abu Jahl cut off one of his hands. Mu'awwidh took his severed hand to God's Messenger. The Messenger stuck the amputated hand onto Mu'awwidh's wrist and applied his saliva to it. It healed at once, and Mu'awwidh returned to the battle and fought until he was martyred.[144] Ibn Wahb reports that during the same battle, Hubayb ibn Yasaf received such a sword blow on the shoulder that it seemed that his shoulder had been split in two. God's Messenger held the parts together, breathed on them, and the wounded shoulder healed.[145]

Although these two Traditions are reported by only one Companion, their occurrence can be regarded as certain, since they happened during a battle that was itself a source of miracles, were verified by such a great authority as Ibn Wahb, and similar incidents also are reported. In fact, nearly 1,000 examples established via authentic narrations indicate that the Messenger healed

---

[144] *Shifa'*, 1:324; 'Ali al-Qari, *Sharh al-Shifa'*, 1:656.

[145] *Shifa'*, 1:324, related by Bayhaqi, Ibn Ishaq, Ibn Kathir, and Ibn Hajar.

wounds.

QUESTION: You qualify many of these Traditions as *mutawatir*, whereas we are hearing most of them for the first time. How could a *mutawatir* Tradition remain unknown for so long?

ANSWER: Many *mutawatir* facts are obvious to religious scholars and unknown to others. Many Traditions that are *mutawatir* to Traditionists may not be regarded by others as even individually reported ones. Axioms or theories in any branch of science are evident only to the authorities of that branch, and others must rely on the authorities or enter that branch to make their own observations. All incidents we have cited so far are regarded as *mutawatir* by Traditionists, scholars of the Shari'a, methodologists, and scholars of many other branches of knowledge, as having the certainty of *tawatur* either in actual wording or in meaning. If the uneducated are unaware of them and if those who blind themselves to the truth do not know them, it is their own fault.

FIFTH EXAMPLE: Imam Baghawi reports and verifies that during the Battle of Khandaq (the Ditch), an unbeliever broke 'Ali ibn al-Hakam's leg. When God's Messenger stroked it, the leg was healed instantly. The soldier continued to fight without even dismounting from his horse.[146]

SIXTH EXAMPLE: Traditionists, mainly Imam Bayhaqi, relate that once 'Ali was very sick. As he was alone and groaning out a prayer for his cure, God's Messenger came in, asked God to heal him, and told him to get up, touching him with his foot. 'Ali was healed at once and later said: "Since then I have never had the same illness."[147]

SEVENTH EXAMPLE: This is the famous story of Shurahbil al-Jufi. A tumor in his palm made it impossible for him to hold his sword and his horse's reins. God's Messenger wiped the tumor and massaged it until no sign of it remained.[148]

EIGHTH EXAMPLE: Six children were honored with the Prophet's miracles. They are as follows:

- Ibn Abi Shayba, a man of perfect character, profound research, and a famous Traditionist, reports: "A woman came to God's Messenger

---

[146] Ibid., 1:323; *Majma' al-Zawa'id*, 6:143; Bayhaqi, 6:185.

[147] Ibn Hanbal, 1:107; *Shifa'*, 1:323; Ibn Hibban, 9:47; Bayhaqi, 6:179.

[148] *Majma' al-Zawa'id*, 8:298, related by Tabarani and Bayhaqi.

with a retarded boy who was mute. God's Messenger rinsed his mouth with water, washed his hands, gave the water to the woman, and told her to have the boy drink it. After the boy had done so, he was cured completely and became so wise and intelligent that he was superior to even the most prudent person."[149]

- Ibn 'Abbas reports that an insane child was brought to God's Messenger. The Messenger put his hand on the child's chest, which caused the child suddenly to vomit a black object resembling a small cucumber. The child was cured instantly.[150]

- Imam Bayhaqi and Nasa'i relate that a boiling saucepan fell on Muhammad ibn Khatib's arm and entirely scalded it. God's Messenger healed the boy by stroking the injured hand and applying his saliva.[151]

- A mute boy came to God's Messenger. When

---

[149] Ibn Maja, no. 3532; Hakim, 2:618; Bayhaqi, 6:82.

[150] Ibn Hanbal, 4:172; Darimi, 1:11-12; also related by Bayhaqi and Tabarani.

[151] Hakim, *al-Mustadrak*, 4:62-63; also related by Tabarani and Bayhaqi.

God's Messenger asked him who he was, the boy said: "You are The Messenger," and began to speak.[152]

- Jalal al-Din al-Suyuti, the leading scholar of his age and who was honored with conversation with God's Messenger many times while awake, related and verified that a newly born baby from Yamama was brought to God's Messenger. When the Messenger turned his face to him, the baby began to speak and said: "I bear witness that you are the Messenger." God's Messenger replied: "May God bless you." After that, the baby never spoke during his infancy. He had been honored with this miracle and the prayer of "May God bless you,"[153] and became famous with the title Mubarak al-Yamama (The Blessed One from Yamama).

- An ill-natured boy interrupted God's Messenger by passing before him while he was praying. God's Messenger said: "O God, let him

---

[152] Ibn Kathir, *al-Bidaya wa al-Nihaya,* 6:158, also related by Bayhaqi.

[153] *Shifa',* 1:319; *Kanz al-'Ummal,* 4:379; Bayhaqi, 6:59.

not leave any traces." After this, the boy was punished for his bad behavior by becoming unable to walk.[154]

- A shameless woman with the mind of a child once asked for a morsel of food which God's Messenger was eating. He gave her one, but she responded: "I want the one in your mouth." God's Messenger gave it to her. After eating it, she became the shyest woman in Madina.[155]

Like these eight, there are perhaps 800 more examples of similar miracles, most of which are recorded in the books of Tradition and his biography. Since his hand was like a drugstore of Luqman, his saliva the life-giving water (elixir) of

---

[154] *Shifa'*, 1:328; Bayhaqi, 5:243; also related by Ibn Hibban. [This incident should not be misunderstood. The Messenger must have discerned that the boy would cause great harm for both himself and the society and, in order to prevent this for the good of both the boy, especially with respect to his eternal life in the Hereafter, and the society, prayed against him. A similar significant incident is related in the Qur'an (18:74, 8 0-81) (Tr.)]

[155] *Majma' al-Zawa'id*, 8:312; *Shifa'*, 1:325; related by Tabarani.

Khadr, and his breath the health-giving breath of Jesus, and since humanity is subject to disease, many people resorted to him. Sick, young, and insane people flocked to him and were cured.

Abu 'Abd al-Rahman al-Yamani (also known as Tawus), one of the greatest Tabi'un scholars and one who made pilgrimage 40 times and performed the morning prayer with ablution of the night prayer for 40 years continuously, stated with certainty: "Whenever an insane person came to God's Messenger, he or she was cured as soon as the Messenger put his hand on his or her chest. There were no exceptions."

As such a great authority, one who lived during the last phase of the Time of Happiness (the time of the Prophet and his four Rightly-Guided Caliphs) had such a definite conviction, it is unquestionable that the Prophet cured everyone who came to him. As this fact became known, we can assume that thousands of people appealed to him.

FOURTEENTH SIGN: Miracles related to the Messenger's prayers also are important. Such miracles are definite and genuinely *mutawatir*, having happened many times. Most of them reach the degree of *tawatur* or are as well-known as the *mutawatir* ones; the rest bear the same certitude as the well-known *mutawatir* Traditions, since they are narrated by the greatest authorities. Of many such instances, we relate only a few that are as famous as, or have the same certainty of, *mutawatir*.

FIRST EXAMPLE: Traditionists, including Imam Bukhari and Imam Muslim, report that God accepted all of the Messenger's prayers for rain immediately. Sometimes it would begin to fall before he lowered his hands while on the pulpit. As mentioned earlier, clouds would appear to meet his army's need for water. Even in his childhood, his grandfather 'Abd al-Muttalib would go with him to pray for rain, and it would come out of respect for him. One of 'Abd al-Muttalib's poems made this famous.

After the Prophet's death, 'Umar once took 'Abbas with him to pray for rain, saying: "O God, this is Your beloved Prophet's uncle. Give us rain for his sake." Thereafter it rained.[156] As reported by Imam Bukhari and Muslim, God's Messenger was asked to pray for rain and did so. It rained so

---

[156] Bukhari, 2:35; Bayhaqi, 6:147.

was asked to pray for rain and did so. It rained so heavily that they asked him to pray for it to cease. He did so, and the rain stopped instantly.[157]

SECOND EXAMPLE: It is as well-known as *tawatur* that even when there were only 40 Companions and they were praying in secret, God's Messenger prayed: "O God, strengthen Islam by 'Umar ibn al-Khattab or 'Amr ibn al-Hisham." A few days later, 'Umar embraced Islam and became a means of openly propagating and exalting Islam.[158] He acquired the sublime title of Faruq (discerning between truth and falsehood).

THIRD EXAMPLE: God's Messenger prayed for various distinguished Companions. His prayers were so readily accepted that they can be considered miracles. The following are some examples out of many:

As reported primarily by Bukhari and Muslim, God's Messenger prayed for Ibn 'Abbas: "O God, make him profoundly knowledgeable in religion

---

[157] *Shifa'*, 1:327, related by Bukhari and Muslim.

[158] Tirmidhi, no. 3684; Ibn Hanbal, 2:95; Hakim, 2:465; Bayhaqi, 2:215.

and teach him the Qur'an's innermost meaning."[159] As a result, Ibn 'Abbas acquired the sublime title of "Interpreter of the Qur'an" and the exalted position of being the "Scholar of the Umma." When Ibn 'Abbas was still young, 'Umar included him in his consultative assembly, which consisted of the Companion's scholars and elders.

Compilers of authentic books of Traditions, including Imam Bukhari, report that Anas' mother asked God's Messenger to pray that Anas would have many descendants and much wealth. He prayed: "O God, give abundance to his wealth and offspring, and bless that which You have bestowed on him." In his old age, Anas swore by God: "I have buried 100 of my children. Concerning my wealth, nobody has lived as happily as I have. You see my abundant wealth, which is due to the Prophet's prayer."[160]

Traditionists, including Imam Bayhaqi, report that God's Messenger prayed for 'Abd al-Rahman ibn 'Awf, one of the ten Companions promised Paradise while still living, to have great wealth. As a result, he gained such wealth that

---

[159] Ibn Hanbal, *Musnad*, 1:264; also related by Bukhari, Muslim, and Hakim.

[160] Bukhari, 8:93, 100; Muslim, no. 2480; Ibn Hanbal, 6:430.

once he gave 700 loaded camels as alms in the way of God.[161] Now reflect on the blessings of the Prophet's prayer and say: "How great are God's blessings."

Tradition narrators, including Imam Bukhari, report that God's Messenger prayed for 'Urwa ibn Abi Ja'da to profit in business. 'Urwa says: "Sometimes I would go to Kufa's market and return home in the evening having earned 40,000 (dirhams)." Imam Bukhari remarks: 'If he had taken a little soil in his hand, he would have gained a profit from it.'"[162] 'Abdullah ibn Ja'far, for whom God's Messenger prayed for abundance, became famous because of his great wealth. He was as well-known for his generosity as he was for his riches.[163]

The above-mentioned miracles are enough to illustrate this point.

Imam Tirmidhi and other Traditionists report

---

[161] *Shifa'*, 1:326; Bayhaqi, 6:218; Abu Dawud, no. 2109.

[162] Bukhari, 4:252; Ibn Hajar, *al-Isaba*, 2:476; Bayhaqi, 6:220.

[163] Ibn Hajar, *Matalib al-'Aliya*, 4077; related by Abu Ya'la and Tabarani.

that God's Messenger prayed for Sa'd ibn Abi Waqqas: "O God, answer his prayer."[164] After that, Sa'd became famous for having his prayers accepted. In addition, everyone feared his malediction. God's Messenger also prayed that Abu Qatada might remain young, saying: "May God prosper your face. O God, bless his hair and skin." When Abu Qatada died at the age of 70, he seemed to be as young as a 15-year-old boy.[165]

Once the poet Nabigha recited his poem in the presence of God's Messenger. When he recited the couplet:

> Our honor and praise have reached the skies; We want to ascend even higher!

the Messenger asked him, jokingly: "To where, O Abu Layla?" He replied: "To Paradise, O Messenger of God." Afterwards, he recited another meaningful poem and the Messenger of God prayed: "May God not deform your mouth." As a result, Nabigha had all of his teeth when he reached the great age of 120 years. Whenever he lost a tooth,

---

[164] Tirmidhi, 3752; Hakim, 3:499; also related by Ibn Hibban and Abu Nu'aym.

[165] *Shifa'*, 1:327, related by Bayhaqi.

a new one would appear in its place.[166]

God's Messenger prayed for 'Ali: "O God, suffice him against heat and cold." As a result, Imam 'Ali felt neither cold nor heat even if he habitually wore winter clothing in summer or summer clothing in winter. He said: "I do not suffer from cold or heat, thanks to the Prophet's prayer."[167] God's Messenger also prayed for Fatima: "O God, do not let her suffer from hunger." Fatima said: "I never suffered from hunger after his prayer."[168]

Tufayl ibn 'Amr once asked the Messenger to perform a miracle for his tribe. The Messenger prayed: "O God, provide light for him." A light appeared between Tufayl's eyes, which was later transferred to the end of a stick. This caused him to be known as Dhu al-Nur (possessor of light).[169]

These are some well-known events that have

---

[166] Ibn Hajar, *al-Isaba*, No. 8639; Bayhaqi, 6:232; Ibn Kathir, *al-Bidaya*, 6:168.

[167] Ibn Hanbal, 1:99; Ibn Maja, 1:43; also related by Bayhaqi and Tabarani.

[168] *Majma' al-Zawa'id*, 9:203, related by Bayhaqi and Tabarani.

[169] *Shifa'*, 1:328, related by Bayhaqi, Ibn Jarir, and Ibn Ishaq.

acquired certitude.

Abu Hurayra complained to the Messenger about forgetfulness. The Messenger told him to spread a piece of cloth on the ground. He then made some movements as if filling his hands with invisible things and emptying them on the cloth. After doing this three or four times, he told Abu Hurayra to pick it up. Thereafter Abu Hurayra, as he later swore by God, never forgot anything.[170]

FOURTH EXAMPLE: Under severe persecution, God's Messenger sometimes had to refer the state of the persecutors to God:

First: The Persian Chosroes, Parwiz, tore up the Prophet's letter. Hearing this, the Prophet prayed: "O God, rend him and his rule as he rent my letter." As a result, Parwiz was killed by his son (Shirwiya) with a dagger, and Sa'd ibn Abi Waqqas tore the Sassanid Empire into pieces, causing it to collapse completely.[171] The Byzantine emperor and the rulers of other states did not perish, for they respected the Prophet's letters.

Second: A famous *mutawatir* Tradition states,

---

[170] Bukhari, 4:253; also related by Muslim, Tirmidhi, and Ibn Hanbal.

[171] Bukhari, 6:10; Abu Nu'aym, *Dala'il al-Nubuwwa*, 2:348.

and Qur'anic verses point out, that in the early days of Islam when God's Messenger prayed at the Ka'ba, the Qurayshi leaders would gather around him and treat him very badly. He had to refer their state to God. Ibn Mas'ud remarks: "I swear by God that I saw all of their corpses after the Battle of Badr."[172]

Third: God's Messenger prayed that the large Mudar tribe would endure famine, since they had contradicted him. Rain stopped, and drought and famine struck them. When the Quraysh, a subclan of the Mudar, asked God's Messenger to pray for rain, he did so and thereby ended the drought and famine.[173] This event is considered *mutawatir*.

FIFTH EXAMPLE: The Prophet's resentment of particular people resulted in their terrible destruction. We cite three examples:

First: He cursed 'Utba ibn Abi Lahab: "O God, send one of your dogs upon him."[174] Some time later when 'Utba was traveling, a lion picked

---

[172] Muslim, 3, no. 1794; Bukhari, 5:94; Ibn Hanbal, 1:417.

[173] Bukhari, 2:37; Bayhaqi, 2:324.

[174] Bayhaqi, 2:335; *Kanz al-'Ummal*, 438-439; Abu Nu'aym, 2:454.

him out in the caravan and tore him up. This very famous event was related and verified by leading Tradition scholars.

Second: God's Messenger dispatched Amir ibn Azbat to command a squadron. Muhallam ibn Jassama killed him out of spite. When God's Messenger learned of this, he became angry and prayed: "O God, do not forgive Muhallam."[175] Muhallam died after 7 days. They put his corpse in the grave, but the grave rejected it. They tried to bury him several times, but each time the grave threw the body out. In the end, a covering finally had to be built.

Third: The Messenger saw a man eating with his left hand. He warned him to eat with his right hand. The man, who felt his pride injured, retorted: "I cannot do so." God's Messenger said: "May you never use it again." After that, he could never raise his right hand again.[176]

SIXTH EXAMPLE: Out of the many wonders manifested through the Prophet's prayer and touch, we mention a few that have acquired cer-

---

[175] *Shifa'*, 1:329; Ibn Hisham, *Sira*, 4:247.

[176] Muslim, no. 2021; also related by Ibn Hibban, Bayhaqi, and Tabarani.

tainty. They are as follows:

First: The Messenger gave Khalid ibn Walid (the Sword of God) a few of his hairs and prayed for his triumph. Khalid kept the hairs in his turban. Due to their worth and that of the prayer, Khalid became victorious in every battle.[177]

Second: Salman al-Farisi was formerly a slave of the Jews. His masters demanded a very high ransom [for his emancipation], saying: "We will emancipate you if you plant 300 date palms and, after they yield fruit, you give us an additional 50 kilos of gold."

Salman explained his situation to the Messenger. God's Messenger planted the date palms somewhere around Madina, and one more was planted by another person. Within the same year, all 300 trees yielded fruit, except for the one planted by the other person. The Messenger pulled it up and replanted it, and it too yielded fruit. He then put some water from his mouth on an egg-sized piece of gold and, after praying, gave it to Salman and told him to give out of it what his masters asked. After Salman did so, it

---

[177] Hakim, 3:289; *Shifa'*, 1:331; Bayhaqi, 6:249.

was still the same size.[178] This miraculous incident, the most significant event in Salman's life, is reported by reliable Traditionists.

Third: A female Companion named Umm Malik used to offer butter to the Messenger out of a leather bag (an *ukka*). He once returned it after praying over it, and told her not to empty or squeeze it. After that, her children would find butter in the bag whenever they wanted some. This continued for a long time, until they squeezed it and ended the blessing.[179]

SEVENTH EXAMPLE: There are many cases of water becoming sweet and emitting a pleasant fragrance, such as:

First: Traditionists, including Bayhaqi, narrate that Bi'r al-Quba (a well) dried up rather frequently. After God's Messenger poured some of his ablution water into it, it always held a great amount of water.[180]

---

[178] Ibn Hanbal, 5:441-42; Ibn Sa'd, *Tabaqat*, 4:53-57; Hakim, 2:16.

[179] Muslim, no. 2280; Ibn Hanbal, 3:242; Bayhaqi, *Dala'il*, 6:113.

[180] *Shifa'*, 1:331, related by Bayhaqi.

Second: Traditionists, above all Abu Nu'aym in his *Dala'il al-Nubuwwa*, report that when God's Messenger put some of his saliva into the well in Anas' house and prayed, its water became the sweetest in Madina.[181]

Third: Ibn Maja narrated that once someone brought a bucket of Zamzam well water to the Messenger. After he put some in his mouth and emptied it into the bucket, the bucket gave off a musk-like smell.[182]

Fourth: Imam Ahmad ibn Hanbal narrates that a bucket of water was taken from a well. After God's Messenger put some of his saliva in the bucket and poured the water into the well, the well began to smell of musk.[183]

Fifth: Hammad ibn Salama, a pious narrator highly esteemed and relied upon by Imam Muslim and the scholars of Muslim West (North Africa and al-Andalus), reports that God's Messenger filled a leather bag with water, breathed a prayer into it, and then tied it up and

---

[181] Ibid., 1:331.

[182] Ibn Maja, no. 659; *Shifa'*, 1:332.

[183] Ibn Hanbal, 22, 67; also related by Ibn Maja.

gave it to some Companions, saying: "Don't open it except for ablution." When they did so, they saw that there was milk inside, with cream on it.[184]

Famous, significant authorities narrate these incidents. Together with those cited here, they show such types of miracles as definitely as *mutawatir* in meaning.

EIGHTH EXAMPLE: Sterile goats gave plenty of milk after the Messenger touched them and prayed. There are various examples of this type of miracle. We mention a few of the best known and most authentic, as follows:

First: All reliable biographies of the Prophet relate that during his migration to Madina, he and Abu Bakr stopped at 'Atiqa bint al-Huda'iyya's house (also known as Umm Ma'bad). She had a very thin, barren goat. When the Messenger asked if the goat produced any milk, she replied: "It does not even have blood in its veins. How can it produce milk?" God's Messenger rubbed its back and loins, stroked its udder, prayed, and then told her to get a vessel and milk her goat. She did so, and God's Messenger, Abu Bakr, and the whole

---

[184] *Shifa'*, 1:334, related by Ibn Sa'd.

household drank until fully satisfied. Following this incident, the goat grew fat and strong and produced lots of milk.[185]

Second: This is the famous story of Ibn Mas'ud's goat. Prior to his conversion, Ibn Mas'ud was a shepherd who cared for the flocks of some Makkan chiefs. One day, God's Messenger and Abu Bakr stopped where he was pasturing the flock. When they asked him for some milk, Ibn Mas'ud replied: "The goats do not belong to me." God's Messenger said: "Bring me a barren goat." Ibn Mas'ud fetched one that had not mated for the past 2 years. The Messenger stroked the goat's udder and prayed. After they milked it and drank its pure, delicious milk,[186] Ibn Mas'ud became a Muslim.

Third: Halima of the Sa'd tribe was the Messenger's wet nurse. Once when her tribe was struck by famine and drought, the animals produced no milk. But when the future Messenger was sent as an infant to be nursed by Halima, her

---

[185] *Majma' al-Zawa'id*, related by Hakim, Bazzar, and Ibn Sa'd.

[186] Ibn Hanbal, 5:210; Ibn Kathir, *al-Bidaya*, 6:102; Ibn Hibban, 8:149.

goats alone, and through his blessing, returned home in the evening fully satisfied and with their udders full of milk.[187]

Although there are similar examples of such miracles in biographies of the Prophet, these few are sufficient for the purpose.

NINTH EXAMPLE: Out of many wonders that happened when the Messenger touched people's heads and faces and then prayed, we relate only a few well-known ones, as follows:

First: He rubbed 'Umar ibn Sa'd's head and prayed. As a result, this man had no white hairs on his head when he died at the age of eighty.[188]

Second: The Messenger stroked part of Qays ibn Zayd's head and prayed. As a result, all of Qays' hair turned gray, except for that area, when he became 100 years old.[189]

Third: 'Abd al-Rahman ibn Zayd ibn al-Khattab was a small, ugly man. The Messenger stroked his head and prayed, after which he

---

[187] *Majma' al-Zawa'id*, 8:220-221, related by Ibn Hanbal, Ibn Hibban, and Ibn Sa'd.

[188] *Shifa'*, 1:334.

[189] Ibid., 1:334.

became almost the tallest and most handsome man.[190]

Fourth: When 'A'iz ibn 'Amr's face was wounded at the Battle of Hunayn, the Messenger wiped the blood away. The part of his face touched by the Messenger became so radiant that Traditionists describe it as "like the whiteness on bay horse's forehead."[191]

Fifth: After he stroked Qatada ibn Salman's face and prayed, it began to shine as brightly as a mirror.[192]

Sixth: Zaynab, daughter of Umm Salama (the mother of believers) and step-daughter of God's Messenger, was a child when he sprinkled some of his ablution water on her face. As a result, her face acquired an extraordinary beauty.[193]

There are many similar examples, most of which are narrated by Traditionists. Taken together, they represent a miracle having the certainty of

---

[190] Ibid., 1:335.

[191] Ibid., 1:334; *Majma' al-Zawa'id*, 9:412, related by Tabarani.

[192] *Shifa'*, 1:334; Ibn Hajar, *al-Isaba*, 3:225.

[193] *Shifa'*, 1:334; related by Tabarani and Ibn 'Abd al-Birr.

mutawatir in meaning, even if we were to regard each one as individual in nature and, accordingly, questionably reported.

Any incident reported in various ways is concluded to have happened, even though the separate reports are individually questionable. Suppose a loud noise is heard. One person says: "Such-and-such a house has collapsed." Another says: "No, a different house has collapsed." A third reports the collapse of a third house, and so on. Each report may be questionable and even untrue, but one thing is certain—a house did collapse. All six examples mentioned above are authentic, and some are famous. Even if we regard each one as questionable, when taken together they prove the occurrence of a miracle, just as the collapse of a house is certain in the above analogy.

Thus each category of miracle cited so far is established firmly, and the individual incidents related illustrate or represent the whole. As the Messenger's hands, fingers, saliva, breath, and prayer are the means of his miracles, other parts of his body (material or immaterial) are the means of many wonders. History books and those relating his biography recount these wonders and display diverse proofs of his Prophethood by expressing his spiritual, moral, and physical qualities.

FIFTEENTH SIGN: Rocks, trees, the moon, and the sun recognize him and testify to his Prophethood, each demonstrating one of his miracles. In the same way, animals, the dead, jinn, and angels recognize him and testify to his Prophethood by becoming the object of his miracles. This sign is explained in three parts, as follows:

FIRST PART: The animal kingdom recognized God's Messenger and became the means for him to work many miracles. We mention only a few of the well-known ones having the certainty of *mutawatir* in meaning, agreed on by exacting authorities, or accepted by the Umma.

First incident: This has the reputation of *mutawatir* in meaning. During the Prophet's migration to Madina, he and Abu Bakr concealed themselves from their pursuers in Thawr cave. Two pigeons guarded its entrance like sentries; a spider, functioning as a doorkeeper, covered the entrance with a thick web.[194]

---

[194] Ibn Hanbal, 1:248; Ibn Kathir, *al-Bidaya wa al-Nihaya*, 3:179-81.

As Ubayy ibn al-Khalaf, a leading Qurayshi who would be killed by the Messenger during the Battle of Badr, was examining the cave, his friends wanted to enter. But he told them: "There's no point. This web seems to have been spun before Muhammad was born." The others added: "Would those pigeons, standing there, still be there if someone were inside?"[195] Ibn Wahb also reports that a group of pigeons shaded the Messenger during Makka's conquest.[196]

'A'isha reports: "We had a pigeon named Dajin in our house. When God's Messenger was at home it would stay quiet, but as soon as he left it would begin to pace to and fro."[197] This signifies that the bird obeyed God's Messenger by remaining quiet in his presence.

Second incident: This concerns a wolf. Such well-known Companions as Abu Sa'id al-Khudri, Salama ibn al-Aqwa', Ibn Abi Wahb, Abu Hurayra, and Uhban (the shepherd directly

---

[195] *Shifa'*, 1: 313, related by Tabarani, Bazzar, and Bayhaqi.

[196] Ibid., 1:313.

[197] Ibid., 1:309, related by Ibn Hanbal, Bazzar, Abu Ya'la, and Bayhaqi.

involved) report this event, which gives it the certainty of *tawatur* in meaning. A wolf once snatched a goat from a herd, but the shepherd rescued the goat. The wolf said: "You deprive me of my food without fearing God." The shepherd muttered: "How strange! Does a wolf speak?" The wolf responded: "What is [really] strange is that a Prophet behind that hill invites you to Paradise, but you do not recognize him!"

All reports agree on the talking wolf. According to Abu Hurayra's report, transmitted through a more reliable channel, the shepherd said to the wolf: "I will go, but who will watch over my goats?" "I will," replied the wolf. The shepherd went to see God's Messenger, leaving the goats under the wolf's care, and soon became a believer.[198] When he returned, he found the wolf watching the goats; not one had been lost. He then slaughtered a goat for the wolf, since it had become his teacher.

Abu Sufyan and Safwan, two leading Qurayshis, once saw a wolf chasing a gazelle. When the gazelle went into the Ka'ba's enclosure, the wolf returned and testified verbally to

---

[198] *Majma' al-Zawa'id*, 8:291, related by Ibn Hanbal.

Muhammad's Prophethood. Surprised, Abu Sufyan warned Safwan: "If we report this miracle to others, I fear all of Makka will join the Muslims."[199] In short, this miracle is certain and *tawatur* in meaning.

Third incident: This is the story of the camel. It is reported through five or six channels by such Companions as Abu Hurayra, Tha'laba ibn Malik, Jabir ibn 'Abdullah, 'Abdullah ibn Ja'far, and 'Abdullah ibn Abi Awfa'.

A camel prostrated before God's Messenger, as if greeting him, and spoke to him. Other reports say that this camel had gone wild in a vineyard, attacking anybody who came near it. When God's Messenger appeared, it came to him, prostrated as a sign of respect, and knelt before him so that the Messenger could put a bridle on it. Then the camel complained to God's Messenger: "They used me in the heaviest work, and now they want to slaughter me, so I went wild." God's Messenger asked its owner if this was true, and he replied that it was.[200]

---

[199] *Shifa'*, 1:311.

[200] Hakim, 2:99; Ibn Hanbal, 3:158; Muslim, 1:268; Ibn Maja, 1:121.

The Prophet owned a camel named Abda'. After the Prophet died, this camel did not eat or drink anything out of grief, and finally died.[201] Such significant authorities as Abu Ishaq al-Isfarani relate that this camel talked with God's Messenger about an important event. Jabir ibn 'Abdullah reports that once his camel became exhausted during a military campaign. When the Messenger prodded it slightly, the resulting joy and agility made the camel move so fast that nobody could catch up with or stop it.[202]

Fourth incident: Traditionists, including Imam Bukhari, relate that one night it was rumored that the enemy was about to attack Madina. Some valiant horsemen set out to investigate. On their way, they saw a man who appeared to be God's Messenger coming toward them. He told them: "There is nothing."[203] He had ridden Abu Talha's horse and investigated the matter before anybody else. He told Abu Talha: "Your horse is very fast and comfortable," although before then it had been

---

[201] *Shifa'*, 1:313.

[202] Bukhari, 7:6; Muslim, 3:1222.

[203] Muslim, no. 2307; Abu Dawud, 4988; Tirmidhi, 1685.

very slow. After that night, no other horse could beat it in a race. On another occasion, the Messenger told his horse to stop so he could pray. The horse remained still until he finished praying.[204]

Fifth incident: Safina, the Messenger's servant, set out to meet Mu'adh ibn Jabal, the governor of Yemen, upon the order of God's Messenger. Encountering a lion on the way, he said to it: "I am the Messenger's servant." The lion made a sound and left without harming him. According to another narration, Safina encountered the lion while returning to Madina. However, he got lost and the lion not only did not harm him but actually showed him the way.[205]

'Umar relates that a Bedouin carrying a lizard said to God's Messenger: "If this animal bears witness to your Prophethood, I will believe in you. Otherwise, I will not." When God's Messenger asked the lizard, it testified verbally to his Prophethood.[206] Umm Salama (a mother of the

---

[204] *Shifa'*, 1:315.

[205] Hakim, 3:606; also related by Bazzar, Tabarani, and Abu Nu'aym.

[206] *Kanz al-'Ummal*, 12:358, related by Bayhaqi, Hakim, and Abu Nu'aym.

believers) reports that an antelope once spoke to God's Messenger and bore witness to His Messengership.[207]

We have cited only a few well-known examples out of many similar ones. We therefore say to those who do not recognize and obey God's Messenger: "Do not try to fall behind the animals after you learn that even wolves and lions recognize and obey God's Messenger."

SECOND PART: Corpses, jinn, and angels recognize God's Messenger. The miracles concerning jinn and angels are *mutawatir* and number in the thousands. Out of many instances illustrating that corpses recognize God's Messenger, we cite only a few related by reliable authorities, as follows:

First: Hasan al-Basri, a devoted student of 'Ali and the greatest Tabi'un religious scholar in Islam's outer and inner dimensions, reported that a bitterly weeping man came to God's Messenger and said: "My little daughter died in that stream nearby, and I left her corpse there." God's Messenger had pity on him, and said: "Come, we will

---

[207] *Shifa'*, 1:314, related by Tabarani, Bayhaqi, Abu Nu'aym, and Ibn Kathir.

go there." They reached the place where she was buried. When God's Messenger called to her, she replied at once: "Here I am, ready to carry out your orders." God's Messenger asked if she wanted to return to her parents. "No," she said, "for I have found a better place here."[208]

Second: Such significant Traditionists as Imam Bayhaqi and Ibn 'Adiyy report that Anas ibn Malik said: "A pious old woman's only son died unexpectedly. She grieved very much and prayed: "O God, I emigrated here only to obtain Your good pleasure and serve Your Messenger, to whom I took the oath of allegiance. For Your Messenger's sake, give me back my son, who was the only one to look after me." Anas says: "That dead son was raised and ate with us."[209]

In his *Qasida al-Bur'a*, written in praise of the Prophet, Imam Busiri refers to this miraculous event:

> If the miracles he worked had been enough
> to demonstrate his unequaled rank,
> Mere mention of his name

---

[208] *Shifa'*, 1:320.

[209] *Al-Bidaya wa al-Nihaya*, 6:292; *Shifa'*, 1:320; Bayhaqi, 6:50.

would suffice to quicken
decayed bones (let alone the newly dead).

Third: Bayhaqi and others quote 'Abdullah ibn 'Ubayullah al-Ansari: "I was present when Thabit ibn Qays ibn Shammas was buried after being martyred during the Battle of Yamama. As he was being buried, people heard him say: 'Muhammad is God's Messenger, Abu Bakr is truthful, 'Umar is a martyr, and 'Uthman is pious and merciful.' We opened the grave only to find him dead."[210] Thabit thus predicted 'Umar's martyrdom even before 'Umar became caliph.

Fourth: Imam Tabarani and Abu Nu'aym in *Dala'il al-Nubuwwa* (Proofs of Prophethood) report from Nu'man ibn Bashir: "Zayd ibn Kharija died unexpectedly at the market. We took his body home. Women cried around him for some time between the evening and the late evening prayers, when he was heard to say: 'Silence, silence!' and continued fluently: 'Muhammad is God's Messenger. Peace be upon you, O Messenger.' We examined him, and found that he was dead."[211]

---

[210] *Shifa'*, 1:320.

[211] *Al-Bidaya wa al-Nihaya*, 6:293; related by Hakim and Bayhaqi.

If living people still do not confirm him even when the dead bear witness to his Messengership, they are more lifeless than corpses and more dead than the dead.

Accounts of angels appearing to and serving God's Messenger, and those of jinn believing in and obeying him, have the status of *mutawatir*, for many Qur'anic verses have affirmed this explicitly. For example, the Qur'an states that during the Battle of Badr, 5,000 angels served him as Companions—like soldiers on the front line. This was done to strengthen the believers' conviction that they would win, not to participate in the battle directly. These angels are distinguished among all others by that honor, just as the people of Badr were distinguished among all other Companions.

There are two aspects to be considered here: The existence of angels and jinn and their relationship with us (decisively proved in The Twenty-ninth Word), and the ability of certain Muslims to see and converse with them through the Messenger's blessing and miracles.

Many Tradition authorities, above all Bukhari and Muslim, report that Archangel Gabriel came to God's Messenger, when he was sitting with some Companions, as a man dressed in white. He asked about belief, Islam, and virtue (*ihsan*), and God's Messenger defined them, thereby teaching the Companions and letting them see the questioner plainly. When the questioner, who appeared to be a visitor although, surprisingly, he bore no signs of travel, suddenly vanished, God's Messenger said: "He was Gabriel, who came to teach you your religion."[212]

Traditionists also report, through authentic narrations having the certainty of *mutawatir* in meaning, that Companions often saw Gabriel with God's Messenger as Dihya, a very good-looking Companion. For instance, 'Umar, Ibn 'Abbas, Usama ibn Zayd, Harith, 'A'isha, and Umm Salama report: "We frequently saw Gabriel with God's Messenger in the form of Dihya."[213] Would they have said this if they could not see Gabriel?

Sa'd ibn Abi Waqqas, conqueror of Persia and one of the ten Companions promised Paradise

---

[212] Bukhari, 1:19-20; *Shifa'*, 1:341, also related by Muslim and many others.

[213] Ibn Hanbal, *Musnad*, 1:212; Bukhari, 4:250; Bayhaqi, 7:52, 87.

while alive, reported: "During the Battle of Uhud we saw two men dressed in white at each side of God's Messenger, as if guarding him. We concluded that they were the Archangels Gabriel and Michael."[214] When such a hero of Islam says he saw them, could he not have seen them?

Abu Sufyan ibn Harith ibn 'Abd al-Muttalib, the Prophet's cousin, reports: "We saw horsemen dressed in white between the sky and Earth during the Battle of Badr."[215] One day, Hamza told God's Messenger that he wanted to see Gabriel. The Messenger complied at the Ka'ba, but Hamza could not bear the sight and fell unconscious.[216]

Several similar instances demonstrate this type of miracle, and indicate that even angels are like moths around his Prophethood's light.

Both Companions and ordinary Muslims can meet and converse with jinn. The most definite example concerns Ibn Mas'ud, whom the Traditionists report through one of the most

---

[214] Muslim, no. 2036; Bukhari, 7:192; Hakim, 2:264.

[215] *Shifa'*, 1:362; Ibn Hanbal, 1:347; related by Bukhari and Bayhaqi.

[216] *Shifa'*, 1:362; Suyuti, *al-Khasa'is al-Kubra'*, 1:311.

authentic narrations, as saying: "I saw the jinn in Batn al-Nakhla on the night they were converted to Islam. They resembled the tall men of the Sudanese Zut tribe."[217]

Another famous incident accepted and narrated by Traditionists concerns Khalid ibn Walid. When 'Uzza (a pre-Islamic idol) was demolished, a female jinn emerged in the form of a dark woman. Khalid cut her into two pieces with his sword. Then God's Messenger said: "They have been worshipping her in the idol 'Uzza. From now on, she will be worshipped no longer."[218]

'Umar said: "When we were with God's Messenger, a jinn named Haama appeared as an old man with a stick. He converted to Islam. God's Messenger instructed him in some short Qur'anic chapters and, after learning his lesson, the jinn departed."[219] Although some Traditionists question this event's accuracy, the outstanding authorities agree that it happened.

---

[217] Ibn Hanbal, 6:165; Suyuti, ibid., 1:343; *Shifa'*, 1:362.

[218] Abu Nu'aym, 2:535; *Shifa'*, 1:362; Ibn Kathir, *al-Bidaya*, 4:316.

[219] Bayhaqi, 5:416; Suyuti, 2:350.

There is no need for long explanations, since we have cited many examples in this respect. However, we add this: Through the light and teaching of God's Messenger, and by following him, thousands of such eminent, godly people of purity as 'Abd al-Qadir al-Jilani have met and conversed with angels and jinn. Thus this event has reached the degree of *tawatur* a hundred times.

THIRD PART: The protection of God's Messenger is an evident miracle, as expressed in: *God will defend you from people* (5:67) and illustrated by many incidents. When God's Messenger proclaimed the Divine Message, he did not challenge just one tribe or race, a few politicians, or a particular religion, but all rulers and all religions. Despite his uncle's and tribe's status as among his greatest enemies, as well as the numerous conspiracies directed against him, he drew his last breath in his own bed in perfect contentment and reached the highest incorporeal realm after 23 years without a guard or any form of protection.

This clearly shows the truth of the above-quoted verse and provides a firm point of support for God's Messenger. In this regard, we mention only a few of the many indisputably certain exemplary events, as follows:

First event: All Traditionists and biographers of the Prophet report that the Quraysh tried to kill him. Advised by a diabolical man or by Satan himself in the form of a man from Najd, they chose at least one man from each clan to avoid any intratribal dispute. Abu Jahl and Abu Lahab led the approximately 200 men who besieged the Messenger's house. 'Ali, who was with God's Messenger that night, was told to sleep in the Messenger's bed. When the Quraysh surrounded the house, the Messenger left and, throwing some dust on them, passed by without being seen.[220]

Second event: God's Messenger and Abu Bakr left Thawr cave, where God had sent a spider and two pigeons to guard them, and set out for Madina. Meanwhile, the Qurayshi chiefs sent Suraqa, a very brave man, to assassinate them in return for a large reward.

Abu Bakr became anxious when they saw Suraqa coming. God's Messenger repeated to him what he had said in the cave: "Don't worry, for

---

[220] *Shifa'*, 1:349; Ibn Hanbal, 4:269; Bayhaqi, 2:465; Abu Nu'aym, 1:202-4.

God is with us." He then glanced at Suraqa, and the hooves of Suraqa's horse got stuck in the ground. Suraqa pulled the horse free and began to follow them, but his horse's hooves got stuck again and he saw smoke arising from that place. Only then did he realize that neither he nor anybody else could lay hands on God's Messenger, and he had to ask for quarter. God's Messenger freed him, saying: "Go back, and make sure nobody else comes."[221]

Also, a shepherd saw God's Messenger and Abu Bakr and hurried to Makka to inform the Quraysh. But when he arrived, he could not remember what he wanted to tell them. Unable to recall anything, he left and only later realized later that he had been made to forget.[222]

Third event: During the military campaign of Ghatfan and Anmar, a courageous chieftain named Ghawras unexpectedly appeared at the Messenger's side. Holding his sword over the Messenger's head, he demanded: "Who will save you from me?" God's Messenger replied: "God."

---

[221] Bukhari, 4:245-46; Muslim, no. 2009; Bayhaqi, 2:483.

[222] *Shifa'*, 1:351; 'Ali al-Qari, *Sharh al-Shifa'*, 1:715.

He then prayed: "O God, protect me from him as You will."

In the same breath, a blow between his shoulders felled Ghawras and his sword slipped from his hand. God's Messenger took the sword and asked: "Now who will save you from me?" God's Messenger then forgave Ghawras and allowed him to return to his tribe. Surprised at such a brave man not doing anything, his fellows asked: "What happened? Why could you not do anything?" He explained what had happened, and added: "I have come from the presence of the best of humanity."[223]

In a similar event, a hypocrite secretly approached God's Messenger from behind during the Battle of Badr. Lifting his sword to strike God's Messenger, at that instant the Messenger turned and glanced at him. This caused him to tremble and drop his sword.[224]

Fourth event: Most interpreters consider this event, almost as well-known as it is *mutawatir*, to be the occasion for revealing:

---

[223] Hakim, 3:29-30; *Shifa'*, 1:348; Bayhaqi, 3:373-79; also by Muslim.

[224] *Shifa'*, 1:347.

> We have put on their necks fetters up to the chin so their heads are raised. We have put before them a barrier and behind them a barrier, and We have covered them so they do not see. (36:9)

Abu Jahl picked up a large rock and swore that he would hit the Prophet with it if he saw him prostrating. Finding the Prophet prostrating, he raised the rock to smash it on the Prophet's head. But his hands froze in the air. God's Messenger finished his prayer and stood up. Only then did Abu Jahl's hands become unbound, either by permission of God's Messenger or because there was no reason for them to remain bound.[225]

In a similar incident, a man from Abu Jahl's clan (Walid ibn Mughira, according to one report) went to the Ka'ba with a large rock to injure God's Messenger while he was prostrating. However, his eyes became sealed and he could not see God's Messenger. Still unable to see (although he could hear), he returned to those who had sent him.[226] When God's Messenger finished his prayer, the would-be assassin's eyes were opened, since there was no need for them to remain closed.

---

[225] Ibid., 1:351; Muslim, no. 2797; Ibn Hanbal, 2:37.
[226] *Shifa'*, 1:351; Bayhaqi, 3:197.

Abu Bakr relates that after *Surat al-Masad*, which begins with *Perish the hands of Abu Lahab* (111:1) was revealed, Abu Lahab's wife, described therein as the *carrier of the firewood* (111:4), picked up a rock and went to the Ka'ba. God's Messenger and Abu Bakr were sitting near it. She could not see God's Messenger and asked Abu Bakr: "Where is your friend? I hear that he satirized me. If I see him, I will hit him on the mouth with this rock!"[227] She could not see the one under God's protection, who was the object of the *hadith qudsi*: "But for you, I would not have created the worlds." And so she could not enter his presence. How could she carry out her plan?

Fifth event: Amir ibn Tufayl and Arbad ibn Qays conspired to assassinate the Messenger. Amir said to Arbad: "I will keep him busy; you hit him." They went to him, but Arbad did not do anything. When Amir later asked him why he had not hit God's Messenger, Arbad replied: "How could I? Every time I intended to hit him, I saw you between us. Did you expect me to hit you?"[228]

---

[227] Hakim, 2:351; Bayhaqi, 2:195.

[228] Bayhaqi, 5:318; *Shifa'*, 1:353; Abu Nu'aym, 1:207.

Sixth event: Either during the Battle of Uhud or Hunayn, Shayba ibn 'Uthman al-Hajabiya approached God's Messenger stealthily from behind. He intended to avenge his father and uncle, who had been killed by Hamza. He lifted his sword, but it suddenly slipped out of his hand. God's Messenger turned to him and put his hand on his chest. When relating this event, Shayba said: "At that moment, no one else was more beloved to me." He embraced Islam instantly, and God's Messenger told him to go and fight. Shayba said: "I fought in front of God's Messenger. If I had I met my own father, I would have killed him."[229]

On the day of Makka's conquest, Fadhala approached God's Messenger with the intent of killing him. God's Messenger smiled at him, asked what he had in mind, and prayed that he might be forgiven. Entering Islam at that moment, Fadhala acknowledged later: "No one in the world was more beloved to me than him at that moment."[230]

---

[229] *Shifa'*, 1:353; Ibn Hajar, *al-Isaba*, 2:157; Abu Nu'aym, 1:195.

[230] *Shifa'*, 1:354; 'Ali al-Qari, *Sharh al-Shifa'*, 1:718.

Seventh event: Some Jews conspired to drop a large rock on the Prophet's head while he was sitting under a particular roof. They were just about to do so when God's Messenger stood up to go. As a result of God's protection, their plot was foiled.[231]

There are many similar instances. Traditionists, above all Imam Bukhari and Muslim, relate from 'A'isha that when *God will protect you from people* was revealed, God's Messenger said to those who had guarded him from time to time: "Leave me, for my Lord, the Mighty and Glorious, protects me."[232]

As this treatise demonstrates, everything in the universe recognizes and is related to God's Messenger, and each displays a specific kind of his miracles. This shows that Prophet Muhammad is the Messenger and envoy of God, the Creator of the universe and the Lord of creation.

An important inspector appointed by the ruler is recognized by every department of the adminis-

---

[231] *Shifa'*, 1:352; also related by Ibn Ishaq and Nasa'i in *al-Khasa'is al-Kubra'*, 1:525.

[232] Hakim, 2:213; Bayhaqi, 2:184; also related by Tirmidhi.

tration and is related to each because he must perform a duty in each department for the ruler. For example, a judicial inspector is connected with the judicial department and is unknown in other departments. Similarly, the civil administration does not recognize a military inspector, and so on.

As proven above, every department of the Divine kingdom, from angels to insects and spiders, knows, recognizes, or has heard of the Messenger of the Lord of the worlds and the seal of the Prophets. And, moreover, the field of his Messengership is far more comprehensive than that of all previous Prophets.

SIXTEENTH SIGN: The wonders that took place before but in connection with his Prophethood are called irhasat. They are of three kinds, as follows:

FIRST KIND: Tidings of Muhammad's Prophethood given by the Torah, Bible, Psalms, and Pages sent to other prophets, as mentioned in the Qur'an. Since they are originally Scriptures revealed by God to His Prophets, it is fitting that they mention the Prophet who would supersede their religions, change the shape of human civilization, and illumine half of the world with the light of Islam. How could these books, which predict even petty events, not mention Muhammad's Prophethood, the most significant phenomenon in human history?

Given that they must do so, the people to whom these Scriptures were sent either would denounce it as falsehood to protect their religions from destruction and their books from annulment, or affirm it so that, via this truthful person, their religions would remain free of superstition and corruption. Both friends and foes agree that their books contain nothing that contradicts or rejects his Prophethood; on the contrary, they affirm it unanimously. Using this, as well as the existence of a definite reason and a fundamental cause for such an affirmation, we will prove this affirmation through three definite evidences.

First evidence: God's Messenger declares to the People of the Book (Jews and Christians) by the tongue of the Qur'an: "Your Scriptures describe and confirm me in whatever I declare." Furthermore, he challenges them with verses such as:

> Say: "Bring the Torah now and recite it,
> if you are truthful." (3:93)

> Say: "Come now, let's call our sons and
> your sons, our women and your women,
> our selves and your selves, and then

> humbly pray and so lay God's curse upon the ones who lie." (3:61)

Despite such strong challenges, no Jewish scholar or Christian priest ever found an error with which to challenge him. If they had, the numerous obstinate and jealous unbelievers of that time, as well as hypocritical Jews and all unbelievers, would have publicized it throughout the land.

Like the polytheists of that time, the Jews and Christians also had to wage war on him when they were not able to contradict him. They chose to fight only to be scattered and forced to emigrate, as they could find no error. If they had, they would have thought themselves saved.

Second evidence: The words of the Torah, Gospels, and Psalms do not have the Qur'an's miraculous perfection. Moreover, many alien terms and ideas have entered them because the translations became far removed from the original texts. Furthermore, the sayings and mistakes, whether intentional or not, of their many interpreters have been confused with the original verses, and the distortions of ignorant people and various enemies have been incorporated. And so these Scriptures suffer from great alteration and corruption.

The famous scholar Shaikh Rahmatullah al-Hindi once silenced priests and Christian and Jewish scholars by proving the thousands of alterations made in those books. Despite this, however, the celebrated scholar Hussain al-Jisri still could extract from them 110 pieces of evidence concerning Muhammad's Prophethood, which he included in his *Risala al-Hamidiya* (translated into Turkish by Ismail Haqqi of Manastir).

Many Jewish and Christian scholars acknowledge that Muhammad's characteristics are recorded in their Scriptures. The Roman emperor Heraclius, a non-Muslim, said: "I agree that Jesus predicted Muhammad's advent."[233] Another Roman ruler, Muqawqis (the governor of Egypt), and other famous Jewish scholars as Ibn Suriya, Ibn Akhtab and his brother Ka'b ibn Asad, and Zubayr ibn Batiya, although remaining non-Muslims, admitted: "Our books mention him and his qualities."[234]

---

[233] Tirmidhi, 2:167; *Shifa'*, 1:364.

[234] *Shifa'*, 1:366, 384; Bayhaqi, 3:361-62; Ibn Kathir, *al-Bidaya*, 4:80-81.

On the other hand, many famous Jewish scholars and Christian monks broke their obstinacy and converted after seeing that Muhammad had the attributes mentioned in their Scriptures concerning the Last Prophet. They silenced some of their former co-religionist scholars by showing them the references in the Torah and the Gospels. Among them were the famous 'Abdullah ibn Salam, Wahb ibn Munabbih, Abu Yasir, Shamul, and Asid and Tha'laba (the two sons of Sa'ya).[235] Shamul lived during the reign of Tubba, ruler of Yemen, and both believed in Muhammad's Prophethood even though his birth was still some time in the future.

Ibn Hayaban once visited the Bani Nadir tribe in Madina before Muhammad announced his Prophethood. He told them: "The emergence of a Prophet is close, and he will emigrate here." Ibn Hayaban died there. When that tribe fought God's Messenger, Asid and Tha'laba publicly called out to them: "By God, he is the one whose coming was promised by Ibn Hayaban."[236] But they ignored the call, and so earned what they earned.

---

[235] *Shifa'*, 1:364; Bayhaqi, 6:240-49; Tirmidhi, 2:206.

[236] Abu Na'im, 1:82; Bayhaqi, 2:80-81.

After seeing the Prophet described in the Torah, many Jewish scholars such as Ibn Bunyamin, Mukhayriq, and Ka'b al-Akhbar converted and thereby silenced those who insisted on disbelief.[237]

And then there is the famous Christian monk Bahira, as mentioned earlier. When he was 12, the Messenger accompanied his uncle on a trading mission to Damascus. From his cell, Bahira noticed that a cloud was shading a certain person in the caravan. He invited all of them to a meal for Muhammad's sake. When he saw that the shade-providing cloud remained where the caravan camped, he thought: "The one I seek must still be there," and so sent a man to fetch whoever was left. When Muhammad was brought, Bahira told Abu Talib: "Return to Makka immediately. The Jews are very jealous and might plot against him, for his description is recorded in the Torah."[238]

Some Nestorians in Abyssinia as well as the Negus (the Abyssinian ruler) embraced Islam together after they found the Prophet described in

---

[237] *Shifa'*, 1:364; Bayhaqi, 3:161-63.

[238] Ibn Sa'd, *Tabaqat*, 1:76; Ibn Hisham, *Sira*, 115; *Shifa'*, 1:308; Hakim, 2:615.

their Scripture.[239] The famous Christian scholar Daghatr also found the Prophet described in the Christians' books and accepted Islam. When he openly declared his conversion to the Byzantines, he was martyred.[240]

A few other examples of such conversions are Harith ibn Abi Shumar al-Ghassani (a Christian leader), Ibn Natur and al-Jarud (prominent religious leaders of Damascus), the ruler of Ilia (in present-day Greece) and Heraclius (Emperor of Byzantium). Heraclius concealed his conversion for the sake of worldly kingdom.[241]

Salman al-Farisi, born a Christian, set out to search for the Prophet after hearing his description.[242] Tamim (a celebrated scholar), as well as the Negus, the Christians of Abyssinia, and the priests of Najran all declared that they found the Prophet described in their books and so believed in him.[243]

---

[239] *Shifa'*, 1:364.

[240] *Shifa'*, 1:364; Bayhaqi, 6:240-49; Tirmidhi, 2:206.

[241] Bukhari, 1:7; Abu Na'im, 1:101-2.

[242] Hakim, 3:604; Ibn Hanbal, 5:437; Ibn Hisham, 1:233.

[243] Shifa', 1:364.

Third evidence: We now point out a few verses from the Gospels, Torah, and Psalms that describe Prophet Muhammad.

First example: In the Psalms we read: *O God, send to us after the interregnum (the latest of the successive prophets) one who will establish (Your) way.*[244] One who will establish (Your) way refers to Prophet Muhammad.

In the Gospels we read: *The Messiah said: I am going to my and your Father so that He may send you the Paraclete* (John 16:7), (that is, Ahmad or Muhammad) and *I will ask the Father, and He will give you another Paraclete to be with you forever* (John 14:16). *Paraclete*, meaning "the distinguisher of truth from falsehood," refers to Prophet Muhammad, as mentioned in those books.[245]

---

[244] Although it does not exist word for word in present editions of the Bible, it is recorded in *Hujjat Allah 'ala al-'Alamin fi Mu'jizat al-Sayyid al-Mursalin* by Yusuf Nahbani, p. 104. (Tr.)

[245] According to *Webster's New World Dictionary*, *Paraclete* derives from the Greek word *parakletos*, meaning "intercessor, advocate, pleader." However Abidin Pasha, a nineteenth-century scholar from Yanya, Greece, who knew Greek very well and whose works on Greek literature were

The Torah says:

> God said to Abraham: "Hagar will bear children. There will appear from her sons one whose hand will be above all, and the hands of all others will be opened to him in reverence."[246]

---

praised highly by Greek authorities, writes that its real origin is *piriklitos*, meaning *Ahmad*, the one who is much praised (Hussain Jisri, *Risala al-Hamidiya*, 59). The Qur'an also states that Jesus predicted Prophet Muhammad with the name Ahmad, a synonym of Muhammad (61:6). Christians assert that Jesus used *Paraclete* for the Holy Spirit. However, what is the Holy Spirit's exact connection with interceding, pleading or advocating, which happen to refer to Prophet Muhammad's main attributes, even though we accept that the word drives from *parakletos*. In addition, Gospel translators prefer to translate *Paraclete* instead of using that word, but all use different terms. In addition, Jesus gives good tidings of the one to come not only as *Paraclete* but also as "the Prince of this world" and "the Spirit of truth," along with many other functions, which must belong to a Prophet and not to a "spirit" or an angel. (Tr.)

[246] Although it does not exist word for word in present versions of the Bible, 'Ali al-Qari records it in his *Sharh al-Shifa'*, 1:743. The Torah says: *I will make the son of the maidservant (Hagar) into a nation* (Genesis, 21:13); *Hagar ... lift the boy up and take him by the hand, for I will make him into a great nation* (21:18). (Tr.)

Another Torah verse reads:

> And He said: "O Moses, I will raise up for them a Prophet like you, from among their brothers (the children of Ishmael). I will put my Word in his mouth, and he will tell them everything I command him. If anyone does not listen to My words that the Prophet speaks in My name, I Myself will call him (or her) to account." (Deuteronomy 18:18-19)

A third Torah verse reads:

> Moses said: "O my Lord, I have found in the Torah a community, as the best of the communities, that will be raised for (the benefit) of humanity. They enjoin good and forbid evil, and believe in God. Let it be my community!" (God) said: "That is the community of Muhammad."[247]

A reminder: In those books, the name Muhammad is given in its Syriac counterparts, such as Mushaffah, Munhamanna, Himyata. The name of Muhammad is mentioned explicitly only in a few places, and envious Jews altered those references.

The Psalms relate:

> O David, a Prophet will come after you, named Ahmad (Muhammad), the Truth-

---

[247] 'Ali al-Qari, ibid., 1:746.

> ful and the Lord, and his community will be forgiven.[248]

'Abdullah ibn 'Amr ibn al-'As, who made extensive studies of earlier Divine books; 'Abdullah ibn Salam, the first famous Jewish scholar to embrace Islam; and Ka'b ibn al-Akhbar, one of the foremost Jewish scholars, all pointed out the following verse in the Torah, which had not yet been corrupted to its present extent. After addressing Moses, the verse addresses the Prophet to come:

> O Prophet, We have sent you as a witness, a bearer of good tidings, a warner and a protection for the unlettered. You are My slave; I have named you "the Reliant on God," who is not harsh and stern, and not clamorous in the marketplaces; who does not repel evil with evil, but instead pardons and forgives. God will not take away his life until He straightens a crooked nation by means of him (by causing them) to proclaim: "There is no deity but God."[249]

Another Torah verse states:

---

[248] Ibn Kathir, *al-Bidaya wa al-Nihaya*, 2:326; *Sharh al-Shifa'*, 1:739.

[249] Bukhari, *Buyu'*, 50; Ibn Hanbal, *Musnad*, 2:174; Darimi, 1:14-15.

> Muhammad is the Messenger of God. His birthplace is Makka. He will emigrate to Tayba. The center of his rule is Damascus, and his community is unceasingly occupied with praising God.[250]

In this verse, a Syriac word meaning Muhammad is actually mentioned for the word Muhammad.

Another Torah verse, *You are My slave and Messenger; I have named you "the Reliant on God,"*[251] is addressed to a Prophet who will emerge, after Moses, from Ishmael's progeny: the cousins of Isaac's children. Also: *My slave is a "chosen one," who is neither harsh nor stern.*[252] "Mukhtar" (chosen one) is a synonym of "Mustafa," one of his names.

The Gospels call the Prophet coming after Jesus "the Master of the world" in several places (John 14:30). Another verse that describes him: *With him is an iron staff with which he will fight, as will his community*,[253] indicates that a Prophet

---

[250] Darimi, 1:14-15; Abu Na'im, *Dala'il al-Nubuwwa*, 1:72.

[251] Kastalani, *al-Mawahib al-Ladunniya*, 6:192.

[252] 'Ali al-Qari, ibid., 1:739.

[253] Yusuf Nahbani, ibid., 105.

will come with a sword to wage jihad. Qur'an 48:29 agrees with this verse, refers to other Gospel verses, and states that his community, like him, will be obliged to wage jihad.

And their similitude in the Gospel is:

> [L]ike a seed that sends forth its blade, then makes it strong; it then becomes thick and stands in its own stem, filling the sowers with wonder and delight, so that it fills the unbelievers with rage at them. (48:29)

In the Torah, a verse says: *The Lord came from Sinai, dawned over them from Seir, and shone forth from Mount Paran* (Deuteronomy 33:2). The Lord came from Sinai refers to Moses' Prophethood, dawned over them from Seir (the Seir mountains are near Damascus) refers to Jesus' Prophethood, and He shone forth from Mount Paran (the Paran mountains of Hijaz) refers to Muhammad's Messengership.[254]

The verse continues, in conformity with the Qur'anic expression: *This is their similitude in the*

---

[254] The Torah calls the place where Hagar stayed with her son (Ishmael) Paran (Genesis, 21:21). The Qur'an calls that place Makka, which was then uninhabited (14: 37). (Tr.)

Torah, says this about the Prophet's Companions who would emerge from Paran's mountains: *The flags of the holy ones are with him, on his right.*[255] This verse describes the Companions as "the holy ones," meaning that they are blessed, righteous, and saintly friends of God.

Isaiah 42 contains the following verses describing Prophet Muhammad, who would come during the last phase of human history:

> Here is my servant, whom I uphold, my chosen one in whom I delight. I will put My Spirit on him, and he will bring justice to the nations. He will not shout or cry out, or raise his voice in the streets. He will not break a bruised reed, and he will not snuff out a smoldering wick. In faithfulness will he bring forth justice; he will not falter or be discouraged till he establishes justice on Earth. The islands will put their hope in his law. (Isaiah 42:1-4)

---

[255] This is almost the same in many versions of the Bible, such as that published by The Bible Company (Istanbul). However, we come across a different translation, if not an alteration, in the Gideon International version: *He came with myriads of holy ones from the south, from his mountain slopes* (Deuteronomy 33:2). (Tr.)

Micah 4 describes Mount 'Arafat and the nation of Muhammad, together with the prayers and praises offered by the pilgrims flocking there from all climes:

> In the last days the mountain of the Lord's temple will be established as chief among the mountains; it will be raised above the hills, and people will stream to it. Many nations will come and say: "Come, let's go up the mountain of the Lord, to the house of God. He will teach us His ways, so that we may walk in His paths." (Micah 4:1-2)

The following verses from Psalms 72 clearly describe Prophet Muhammad:

> He will rule from sea to sea and from the river to the ends of Earth. The desert tribes will bow before him, and his enemies will lick the dust. The kings of Tarshish and of distant shores will bring tribute to him; the kings of Yemen and Seba will present him gifts. All kings will bow to him, and all nations will serve him, for he will deliver the needy who cry out, the afflicted who have no one to help. He will take pity on the weak and the needy, and save the needy from death. He will rescue them from oppression and violence, for precious is

> their blood in his sight. Long may he live! May people ever pray for him and bless him all day long.... May his name endure for ever. May it continue as long as the sun. All nations will be blessed through him, and they will call him blessed. (Psalms 72:8-17)

Since Prophet David, has there been another Prophet other than Prophet Muhammad who spread his religion from east to west, to whose name many rulers pay tribute, whose way so many people obey out of deep adoration for him, and on whom one fifth of humanity daily calls God's peace and blessings?

John 16:7 reads: *It is for your good that I am going away. Unless I go away, the Comforter will not come to you.* Who other than Prophet Muhammad could be humanity's true comforter? Certainly he is humanity's pride and comforter by saving all people who follow him from eternal annihilation.

John 16:8 reads: *When he comes, he will convict the world of guilt in regard to sin and righteousness and judgment.* Who, other than Prophet Muhammad, came and transformed the disorder prevailing at his time into goodness and harmony to save the world from sin and polytheism and to revolutionize its politics and rule?

John 16.11: *...and in regard to judgment, because the Prince of the World has been judged already.* This "Prince" is Prophet Muhammad, since he is known as the Master of Humanity. Indeed, he is such a prince that many millions of people have followed him in each of the 14 centuries since he lived. They obey his commands willingly and daily renew their allegiance to him by calling God's blessings upon him.

John 16:12-13 reads:

> I have much more to say to you, more than you can now bear. But when he, the Spirit of truth comes, he will guide you into all truth. He will not speak on his own but will speak only what he hears, and he will tell you what is to come.

These verses are quite clear. Other than Prophet Muhammad, who invited everyone to the truth, always spoke what he heard from God (through Gabriel) so that each of his words is based on Divine revelation, and informed people in detail about the Day of Judgment and the Hereafter?

In the books of other Prophets, God's Messenger is mentioned with various Syriac and Hebrew names corresponding to Ahmad, Muhammad, and Mukhtar. The Pages of the Prophet Shu'ayb call him Mushaffah (Muhammad). The Torah mentions him as Munhamanna (Muhammad) and Himyata ("the Prophet of al-Haram"). The Psalms call him al-Mukhtar ("the Chosen One"), the Torah call him al-Hatam al-Khatam, and both refer to him as Muqim al-Sunna ("the one who establishes and enforces the Divine way for humanity"). The Pages of Abraham and the Torah mention him as Mazmaz, and elsewhere the Torah calls him Ahyad.

God's Messenger said: "In the Qur'an my name is Muhammad, in the Bible Ahmad, and in the Torah Ahyad." In the Bible, he is referred to as "the Possessor of the Sword and the Staff." Of all those Prophets who carried the sword, Prophet Muhammad, whom God told to perform jihad with his community, is the greatest. The Gospel also calls him "the one who wears a crown." This refers to a turban,[256] and the Arabs have worn headcovers with a wrapper around them since

---

[256] The Muslim turban signifies loftiness or exaltation. If a Muslim dreams of wearing a turban, this is interpreted as either his greatness or that he will hold an exalted post. (Tr.)

ancient times. Hence the reference is undoubtedly to Prophet Muhammad.

Biblical interpreters define *Paraclete* (or *Faraclete*) as "the one who distinguishes truth from falsehood," meaning the one who guides future generations of humanity to the right path. Jesus is quoted as saying in the Gospel that he must leave so that the Prince of the World will come. After Jesus, who other than Prophet Muhammad came as the leader of humanity, distinguished truth from falsehood, and guided humanity? Jesus always told his people: "One will come, and [after that] there will be no need for me. I am his forerunner and bring good tidings of his coming." This is confirmed by the Qur'an:

> And remember, Jesus, the son of Mary, said: "O Children of Israel, I am a Messenger of God unto you, confirming what was revealed before me in the Torah and bringing the glad news of a Messenger who will come after me, whose name is Ahmad." (61:6)

In Shamun al-Safa's tomb, the famous traveler Awliya' Calabi saw the following Gospel verses written on a gazelle hide:

> *'Itun Azribun peruftun. Law ghislin. Bent afzulat; ki kalushir; tunuminin mavamid. Isfedus takardis, bist bith.* (A youth from Abraham's progeny will be a Prophet. He will not be a liar. His birthplace is Makka; he will come with righteousness; his blessed name is Ahmad Muhammad. His followers will prosper in this world and also in the next.)[257]

The Gospels record Jesus' frequent glad tidings of the coming of humanity's most significant leader and mention him with some Syriac and Hebrew names meaning, as observed by meticulous experts, Ahmad, Muhammad, and Faruq (one who distinguishes truth from falsehood).

Question: Why did Jesus give good tidings of the Last Prophet's coming more emphatically than the other Prophets who predicted him?

---

[257] The language referred to must be Syriac, as many Syriac people still live in south-eastern Turkey, where many Christian saints—true, monotheist followers of Jesus—are buried. Interestingly enough, due to the studies and endeavors of such monotheist Christian scholars as Arius, Eastern Christians were usually monotheists and so easily accepted Islam. Western Christianity, on the other hand, insisted upon retaining the doctrine of the Trinity and other borrowed creeds. (Tr.)

Answer: Prophet Muhammad declared Jesus' purity against the Jews' slanders, defended him against their denial, and purified Jesus' way of its great alteration and corruption. In addition, instead of the Jews' burdensome religious law, he presented a feasible and all-encompassing religion with an exalted law that completed the law of Jesus' religion. This is why Jesus often announced the glad tidings that "the Leader of the World is coming."

As explained earlier, the Torah, Gospels, Psalms, and Pages of other Prophets contain numerous emphatic mentions of a promised Prophet who is to come and mention him with various names. Since this Prophet is mentioned in all Prophetic books, who else could he be other than Muhammad, the Prophet who came in the last phase of human history?

SECOND KIND: The second kind of *irhasat* includes the predictions of Prophet Muhammad's coming by soothsayers and Gnostics living in the period between Jesus and Muhammad's Prophethood. To a certain degree, they were considered the saints of their times. They predicted his coming in verse and entrusted them to later generations. There are many such instances, but we mention only a few well-known ones that have been accepted and transmitted by historians and the Prophet's biographers.

First example: Tubba, a Yemeni ruler, saw the Messenger's qualities in the previous Scriptures, believed in him, wished to occupy the same place as 'Ali, and proclaimed his belief in the following couplet:

> I bear witness to Ahmad
> that he is a Messenger from God,
> the Creator of humanity;
> Were I to live long enough to see him,
> I would be a minister and
> like a cousin to him.[258]

Second example: Quss ibn Sa'ida was the most famous and significant Arab orator, in addition to being an enlightened monotheist. Before Muhammad was raised as a Prophet, he announced Muhammad's Messengership with these verses:

> Among us (God) sent forth Ahmad
> as the best Prophet ever raised,
> Upon him be God's blessings.[259]

---

[258] Hakim, 2:388; *al-Bidaya wa al-Nihaya*, 2:166.

[259] *Shifa'*, 1:363; *al-Bidaya*, 2:230; Bayhaqi, 2:101.

Third example: Ka'b ibn Lu'ayy, one of the Messenger's ancestors, announced Muhammad's Prophethood through inspiration:

> In the time of heedlessness
> Muhammad will appear suddenly;
> He will give tidings that are all true.[260]

Fourth example: The Yemeni ruler Sayf ibn Dhiyazan saw the Messenger's description in the previous Scriptures, believed in him, and loved him very much. When 'Abd al-Muttalib (the Messenger's grandfather) arrived in Yemen with a Qurayshi trade caravan, Sayf summoned them and said: "A child will be born in the Hijaz with a mark between his shoulders that looks like a seal. He will be the leader of humanity." In private, he told 'Abd al-Muttalib: "You are his grandfather,"[261] thus predicting Muhammad's Prophethood in a miraculous way.

Fifth example: God's Messenger was worried when the first Revelation came to him. His wife Khadija told Waraqa ibn Nawfal (her paternal cousin) what had happened, and he told her to send Muhammad to him. God's Messenger went

---

[260] *Al-Bidaya*, 2:244; *Shifa'*, 1:364.

[261] Hakim, 2:388; *al-Bidaya*, 2:328; *Shifa'*, 1:143.

to Waraqa and told him about the Revelation. Waraqa said: "Good tidings to you, O Muhammad. I bear witness that you are the expected Prophet, and that Jesus has given glad tidings about you."[262]

Sixth example: The Gnostic Askalan al-Himyeri always asked any Qurayshis he met: "Does someone among you claim Prophethood?" The people always replied in the negative. After Muhammad declared his Prophethood, he asked them the same question and was told that there was such a person. He responded: "This is the one for whom the world has been waiting for so long."[263]

Seventh example: The renowned Christian scholar Ibn al-A'la predicted the Prophet before his declaration of Prophethood and without seeing him. When he finally met the Prophet, he said: "By the One Who sent you with the truth, I found your description in the Gospel, and the Virgin Mary's son gave glad tidings about you."[264]

---

[262] Ibn Hanbal, 4:304; Bukhari, 1:3.

[263] *Shifa'*, 1:363.

[264] 'Ali al-Qari, *Sharh al-Shifa'*, 1:744.

Eighth example: Abyssinia's Negus, cited earlier, said: "I wished I had been in his service rather than in possession of this kingdom."[265]

In addition to those Gnostics who gave tidings of the future by basing their knowledge on Divine inspiration, those soothsayers who were allowed (until the Prophet's time) to obtain tidings of the Unseen and the future via spirits and jinn also predicted his coming and Prophethood. We cite only a few of many such cases that enjoy the certainty of *tawatur* in meaning and are recorded in many history books and biographies of the Prophet.

First example: Shiqq, a famous soothsayer who looked like half a man with one eye, one hand, and one leg, repeatedly predicted Muhammad's Messengership. His reports are recorded in history books with the certainty of *tawatur* in meaning.[266]

Second example: Satih, the famous soothsayer of Damascus, was a monstrosity who almost lacked bones, even limbs, and with a face that looked like a part of his breast. He lived a long life

---

[265] *Shifa'*, 1:364; Bayhaqi, 2:285.

[266] Abu Na'im, *Dala'il al-Nubuwwa*, 1:123; *Shifa'*, 1:365.

and was highly reputed for his true predictions. Chosroes of Persia sent the learned envoy Mubazan to him to interpret a strange dream that showed 14 pinnacles of his palace collapsing (on the night of Muhammad's birth). Satih said: "From now on, your country will have 14 rulers and then be destroyed utterly. A man will appear to preach a religion. He will abolish both your rule and religion,"[267] a clear reference to the Last Prophet's coming.

Such famous soothsayers as Sawad ibn Qarib al-Dawsi, Khunafar, Af'a Najran, Jizl ibn Jizl al-Kindi, Ibn Khalasat al-Dawsi, and Fatima bint Nu'man al-Najjariya also had their predictions recorded in history books and biographies of the Prophet. They predicted his coming and that he would be Muhammad.[268] Sa'd ibn bint al-Kurayz, 'Uthman's relative, learned of Muhammad's Prophethood through divination and, in the early days of Islam, told 'Uthman to go and believe. 'Uthman did so, and Sa'd expressed this in the following couplet:

---

[267] Bayhaqi, 2:126-129; *Shifa'*, 1:365.

[268] Bayhaqi, 2:248; *al-Bidaya*, 2:335; *Shifa'*, 1:365.

> Through my words, God guided
> 'Uthman to that thing,
> By means of which is his perfection.
> Truly God guides to the truth![269]

The jinn call their soothsayers *hatif*. They cannot be seen, but they can be heard. These beings repeatedly foretold the coming of God's Messenger. A few of the *hatifs*' well-known and many tidings and messages are as follows:

- A *hatif* brought Dhayab ibn al-Harith and others to Islam by calling to him loudly:

  > O Dhayab, O Dhayab, listen to the oddest thing:
  > Muhammad was sent with the Book.
  > He is calling in Makka,
  > yet they do not accept him.[270]

- Another *hatif* called out to Sami'a ibn Qarrat al-Qatafani:

  > The truth has come and become bright;
  > Falsehood has been destroyed
  > and become uprooted,[271]
  > and caused the conversion of some people.

Idols and even animals offered to idols also proclaimed Muhammad's Messengership by

---

[269] Suyuti, *al-Khasa'is al-Kubra'*, 1:258.

[270] Ibid., 1:358.

[271] *Sharh al-Shifa'*, 1:748.

God's power and permission. For example, the Mazan tribe's idol told them of Muhammad's declaration of Messengership by crying out: "He is the Prophet who has been sent. He has come with the revealed truth."[272] 'Abbas ibn Mirdas was converted by an idol named Dimar. One day, that idol was heard to say: "Dimar was worshipped before the true message of Prophet Muhammad. Now Dimar's time is over."[273] Before his conversion, 'Umar heard a sacrifice offered to idols say: "O sacrificer, the means of prosperity are at hand. An eloquent man is declaring: 'There is no deity but God.'"[274]

There are many more such instances, all of which are narrated in authentic reports in reliable books.

In addition, various rocks, grave sites, and gravestones were found to bear, inscribed in earlier scripts, such passages as "Muhammadun Muslihun Amin" (Muhammad, a reformer, a trustworthy one). Some people were converted

---

[272] Ibn 'Abd al-Birr, *al-Isti'ab*, 3:446; *al-Bidaya*, 2:337.

[273] *Al-Bidaya*, 2:341-42; Bayhaqi, 1:118.

[274] Bukhari, 5:61; *al-Bidaya*, 2:332.

through such events.[275] Such passages can refer only to God's Messenger, for during the time just before his birth there were only seven Muhammads, none of whom deserved to be or was ever designated "the reformer" or "the trustworthy one."

THIRD KIND: This includes the wonderful events at the time of and in connection with the Messenger's birth. Many other incidents occurred before he was commissioned with Messengership, and each is one of his miracles. Out of many examples, we mention a few that became very well-known and accepted by Tradition authorities as having verified authenticity.

First example: On the night of his birth, the Prophet's mother and the mothers of 'Uthman ibn al-'As and 'Abd al-Rahman ibn al-'Awf saw a magnificent light. Each woman said: "During his birth, we saw a light that illuminated the east and the west."[276]

---

[275] Ibn Hanbal, 4:215; *Shifa'*, 1:467; Ibn Sa'd, *Tabaqat*, 4:215.

[276] *Shifa'*, 1:366; Ibn Sa'd, ibid., 1:63; Bayhaqi, 1:80-92; Hakim, 2:600.

Second example: On that night, idols within the Ka'ba toppled over.[277]

Third example: During that night, Chosroes' palace shook and cracked, and its 14 pinnacles collapsed.[278]

Fourth example: On that night, the small lake of Sawa in Persia (sanctified by the Persians) sank into Earth. The fire worshipped by the Magians at Istakhrabad, which had burned continually for 1,000 years, went out.[279]

These incidents indicated that person born on that night would abolish fire-worship, destroy the palace of the Persian rulers, and prohibit the sanctification of things that God does not allow to be sanctified.

Fifth example: Incidents taking place before the night of his birth also are considered *irhasat*. Of these, the Event of the Elephant (105:1-5) is the best known. Abraha, governor of Yemen for the Abyssinian kingdom, marched upon Makka to destroy the Ka'ba. He placed his huge elephant

---

[277] Bayhaqi, 1:19.

[278] Abu Nu'aym, 1:139; Bayhaqi, 1:126.

[279] Suyuti, *al-Khasa'is*, 1:128; *Shifa'*, 1:366.

Mahmud at the front of his army. When they approached Makka, the elephant stopped. Since they could not make it move forward, they retreated. On their way, a host of *ababil* birds attacked and routed them.

This curious event is recorded in history books. It is also a sign of Muhammad's Prophethood, for this miraculous event saved the Ka'ba and Makka, his birthplace and beloved home and toward which he would pray. This happened at a time close to his birth.

Sixth example: When God's Messenger was residing with Halima's Family during his childhood, both Halima and her husband often observed a small cloud shading his head.[280] They narrated this event, and it acquired a justified fame.

Similarly, when he traveled to Damascus at the age of 12 with his uncle, the Christian monk Bahira saw and pointed out to others a small shade-providing cloud located above Muhammad.[281] Before his Prophethood, Khadija noticed that two

---

[280] Ibn Sa'd, *Tabaqat*, 1:97; Ibn Kathir, *al-Bidaya*, 2:273; *Shifa'*, 1:368.

[281] Abu Nu'aym, *Dala'il*, 1:168-172; Tirmidhi (version verified by Tuhfat al-Ahwazi, No. 3699); Ibn Hisham, 1:180-81.

angels, in the form of a cloud, shaded God's Messenger when he returned from a trading journey with her servant Maysara. When she mentioned this to Maysara, the latter responded: "I saw the same throughout the journey."[282]

Seventh example: An authentic narration reports that before his Prophethood, God's Messenger once sat under a tree. That previously arid spot suddenly became green, and the tree's branches bent down and twisted above his head to shade him.[283]

Eighth example: God's Messenger stayed with Abu Talib during his boyhood. Whenever Abu Talib and his household ate with him they were satisfied; when he did not eat with them they were not satisfied.[284] This is a well-known and authenticated incident. Umm Ayman, who served God's Messenger when he was a child, reports: "He never complained about hunger and thirst, neither when he was little nor when he grew up."[285]

---

[282] *Shifa'*, 1:368; Bayhaqi, *Dala'il al-Nubuwwa*, 2:65.

[283] *Shifa'*, 368; *Sharh al-Shifa'*, 1:753.

[284] Abu Nu'aym, 1:166; *Shifa'*, 1: 367.

[285] *Shifa'*, 1:368; Bayhaqi, 6:125; Suyuti, *al-Khasa'is*, 1:111.

Ninth example: The milk of his wet nurse's (Halima) goats and goods were seen (unlike others in the tribe) to increase through his blessing.[286] Also, flies did not bother him.[287] One of his descendants, Sayyid 'Abd al-Qadir al-Jilani, inherited this quality.

Tenth example: After the Messenger's birth, and especially during the night of his birth, shooting stars became more frequent. This was a sign that satans and jinn could no longer obtain knowledge of the Unseen.[288]

Since God's Messenger would be endowed with Revelation, any information about the Unseen given by soothsayers and jinn, which is usually inaccurate and mixed with falsehood, would have to cease. This was necessary so that people would not mistake such words for Revelation or doubt the Revelation itself. The Qur'an ended soothsaying, which was widespread before Muhammad was raised as the Prophet. Many soothsayers embraced Islam, for they could find

---

[286] *Al-Bidaya*, 2:273; Ibn Hisham, 1:173; *Shifa'*, 1:366.

[287] *Shifa'*, 1:368.

[288] *Shifa'*, 1:347-48.

no jinn informers to provide them with information of the Unseen.[289]

To conclude, many incidents and people confirmed, or caused others to confirm, Muhammad's Prophethood. All creation, both as an individual and as a species, longingly waited for and announced, with God's permission, the advent of the world's spiritual leader.[290]

This leader would change the world's spiritual and moral structure, make it the sowing ground for the Hereafter, proclaim the real value of the world's beings, save transient humanity and jinn from eternal annihilation, disclose the Divine purpose for the universe's creation, and make the

---

[289] Today, soothsaying has reappeared in the form of mediumship. However, that topic is beyond the scope of this book.

[290] This being, who was addressed by God with the words "But for you, I would not have created the worlds," is so great a leader that his rule continues even after 14 centuries. In each century since he lived, millions of people and half the globe have placed themselves under his banner. His subjects, who today number more than 1.5 billion, try to follow him in deep respect and daily ask God to bestow peace and blessings upon him. Thus they daily renew their oath of allegiance to him.

Creator known to everybody. As proved in the previous signs and examples, each species of creation welcomed him by becoming the means for him to work one variety of his miracles, thereby affirming his Prophethood.

SEVENTEENTH SIGN: After the Qur'an, the Messenger's greatest miracle is his character and person, his moral example. Friend and foe alike agree that he possessed the highest level of all moral virtues. 'Ali, a man of the greatest bravery, repeatedly said: "In the fiercest phases of fighting we would withdraw into the stronghold of God's Messenger and take refuge behind him." Likewise, he possessed all laudable characteristics to the highest degree. For this greatest miracle, we refer readers to Qadi 'Iyad's *Shifa' al-Sharif*, which beautifully explains and proves the Prophet's miraculous moral character.

Another great miracle, also affirmed by friend and foe, is his supreme Sacred Law (the Shari'a), the like of which never came before and will never come again. For a partial explanation of this supreme miracle, consult our writings, especially the 33 Words, 33 Letters, 33 Gleams, and 13 Rays.

One of the Messenger's certain and *mutawatir* miracles is splitting the moon by a gesture of his index finger. This miracle, reported by some of the foremost Companions (e.g., Ibn al-Mas'ud, Ibn 'Abbas, Ibn 'Umar, Imam 'Ali, Anas, and Khudayfa), was proclaimed to the world by: *The Hour is near, and the moon split* (54:1). The stubborn Qurayshi polytheists did not contradict the news, but claimed that it was magic. Thus even unbelievers testify to its occurrence. His Mi'raj (Ascension) is a still greater miracle shown to the heavens' inhabitants. Readers can refer to the Treatise of the Mi'raj, a short part of which appears at the end of this treatise as an appendix. We will mention another miracle that the Prophet worked in connection with the Mi'raj.

When God's Messenger informed the Quraysh of this event, they refused to believe him, saying: "If you actually traveled to the Masjid al-Aqsa in Jerusalem, as you claim, describe its doors and walls." God's Messenger would later say: "I was annoyed by their question and denial in a way that had never happened to me before. Suddenly, God lifted the veil between me and Bayt al-Maqdis (Masjid al-Aqsa) and showed it to me. I looked at it and described it as it stood before my eyes."[291] Thus the Quraysh realized that God's Messenger was giving the correct and complete description.

In addition, God's Messenger told them: "During my journey I saw one of your caravans. It will arrive here tomorrow at such and such a time." The Quraysh waited for its arrival at the promised time. It seems the caravan was about to be delayed by about an hour. In order for the Prophet's word to be proved true, Earth did not rotate for one hour.[292] This is confirmed by meticulous researchers.

Considering that Earth stopped rotating to confirm Prophet Muhammad's words, and that the sun witnessed this by its apparent rest in the sky, just imagine how vast is the misfortune of those who do not confirm and follow such a person, and how vast is the good fortune of those who respond: "We have heard and obeyed" and proclaim: "Thanks be to God for belief and Islam."

---

[291] Muslim, 1:156-57; Tirmidhi, No. 3133; Bukhari, 5:66; Ibn Hanbal, 3:378.

[292] 'Ali al-Qari, *Sharh al-Shifa'*, 1:704; Bayhaqi, *Dala'il al-Nubuwwa*, 2:404.

EIGHTEENTH SIGN: The Messenger's greatest and eternal miracle is the Qur'an, which encompasses hundreds of proofs of his Prophethood and whose 40 miraculousness aspects have been proved.[293] Here we mention only a few significant points in this respect, as follows:

FIRST POINT: QUESTION: The Qur'an's miraculousness mainly lies in its eloquence, which can be comprehended only by one out of a thousand discerning scholars. Should not everyone be able to glimpse this miraculousness according to their own understanding?

ANSWER: The Qur'an has a different kind of miraculousness for everyone and indicates this in the most perfect way. To people of eloquence and rhetoric, it shows its miraculous eloquence; to poets and orators, it displays its miraculous and uniquely exalted style, one that cannot be imitated although it is liked by everyone. The passage of time does not effect its freshness, so it is always new. Its metrical and rhythmical prose and its verse have the greatest nobility and charm.

---

[293] See Said Nursi, *The Words*, vol. 2 (Turkey: The Light, Inc., 2002).

To soothsayers and foretellers, the Qur'an's miraculousness consists of the reports it gives about the Unseen. To historians and chroniclers, its miraculousness is the news it relates about past nations, future conditions and events, and the Intermediate World and the Hereafter. To social and political scientists, it presents the miraculousness of its sacred principles, which comprise the Shari'a. To those engaged in the knowledge of God and the Divine laws of nature, its miraculousness in shown its sacred Divine truths. To those following a spiritual way to sainthood, it manifests the profound, manifold meanings in its verses that rise in successive motions like waves of the sea.

In short, the Qur'an shows its 40 aspects of miraculousness to everyone by opening a different window. Even those who just listen to it and can derive a very limited meaning from it agree that the Qur'an sounds like no other book. Any ordinary person who listens to it says: "This Qur'an is either below other books in degree—which is utterly impossible, and which even its enemies [and Satan] do not claim—or above them all and therefore a miracle." Now, we explain the aspect of miraculousness perceived by an ordinary person who simply listens to it.

The miraculous Qur'an challenges the world and stirs up two kinds of feelings: First, its friends desire to imitate its style and to speak and write like their beloved Qur'an. Second, its enemies acquire a passion to criticize and dispute, and to nullify its claim of miraculousness by competing with its style. As a result, millions of books have been written in Arabic—and we still have them. Whoever listens to even the most eloquent and rhetorical of them will say that the Qur'an sounds like none of them.

Another miraculous aspect that it shows to illiterate people is that its recitation does not bore anyone. An illiterate person, even one who does not comprehend the Qur'an's meaning, undoubtedly would say upon hearing it recited: "If I hear a most beautiful and famous couplet two or three times, it starts to bore me. But this is not true with the Qur'an, for the more I listen, the more pleasant it becomes. It cannot be a human composition."

The Qur'an shows its miraculousness even to children learning it by heart. Although its many similar verses and passages might cause confusion, children memorize it easily even though they cannot retain one passage about something else for long. For those who are sick and close to death, who are disturbed by the slightest noise, the Qur'an's recitation and sound becomes as sweet and comforting as the water of Zamzam, thereby displaying another aspect of its miraculousness. For those who can see but cannot hear or learn, one of the almost 40 classes of people to whom the Qur'an shows its miraculous qualities without depriving any of them, there are other signs.[294]

---

[294] For example, Hafiz 'Uthman's copy has many related words corresponding to each other on different pages. If the sheets beneath *their dog being the eighth* (*Surat al-Kahf*) are pierced, with a slight deviation it will go through *Qitmir* (*Surat al-Fatir*), thus giving the dog's name. *Mukhdarun* and *mukhdarin* (they will be brought before us) in *Surat al-Saffat* correspond to each other and to the one found in *Sura Ya Sin* twice, one below the other. *Mathna* (in pairs) occurs three times in the Qur'an; that the two of them correspond to each other, one at the beginning of *Surat al-Fatir* and the other toward the end of *Sura Saba'*, cannot be by chance.

Many similar examples exist. Sometimes the same word occurs almost in the same place on five or six pages. I once saw a Qur'an in which similar passages, written in red ink, faced each other on facing pages. This pointed to another kind of miracle. Later, I noticed many more passages on various pages significantly facing each other. Since the Qur'an's verses and chapters were arranged at the Prophet's direction and later on copied through Divine inspiration, its

SECOND POINT: As magic was widespread during Moses' time, his miracles were of that kind. As medicine was in demand during Jesus' time, his miracles were of that kind. When Muhammad was

---

design and calligraphy are miraculous. Any deviation is the result of human acts.

Also, each long or medium Madinan *sura* repeats *Allah* in a very significant manner: five, six, seven, eight, nine, or eleven times on both sides of a sheet or on two facing pages—a beautiful and significant numerical proportionate.

Although the Qur'an has all the features of persuasive eloquence (e.g., rhythm, rhyme, and artistic style) that capture our attention, it always provides sublime seriousness, serenity of mind, and the peace of being in His presence to those who remember and supplicate God. Other kinds of persuasive eloquence often disturb, for their elegance intrudes upon one's peace of mind and undermines seriousness and inward concentration.

For the last 8 or 9 years I have read Imam Shafi'i's famous supplication daily. Although it is the most graceful, meaningful, and eloquent one of its kind, and even ended a season of drought and famine in Egypt, I came to see that its rhymed and metrical wording interrupts the supplication's solemnity. Thus I deduced that the Qur'an's miraculously genuine, natural, matchless, and unique rhythm and rhyme preserves peace and solemnity. Those who remember and supplicate God feel this miraculousness in their hearts, even if their minds do not realize it.

Another miraculous aspect is that it shows the highest and brightest degree of belief possessed by God's Messenger,

raised as a Prophet, four arts were popular in Arabia: eloquence and fluency in writing and speaking, poetry and oratory, soothsaying and divination, and knowledge of the past and cosmology.

When the miraculous Qur'an came, it challenged all experts in these four fields. First, it brought people of eloquence to their knees as they listened to it in total admiration. Second, it shocked poets and orators so much that they bit

---

the object of the Greatest Divine Name's display. Like a sacred map, it details the sublime truths of the Hereafter and the Lord's kingdom and shows us, in a natural way, how exalted is the true and comprehensive religion of Islam.

It also conveys the address of the universe's Creator as the Lord of creation, with all His glory and majesty. Therefore, as the Qur'an states: *Say: If all humanity and jinn were to come together to produce the like of this Qur'an, they could not produce the like of it* (17:88). All such attempts are worth almost nothing in comparison, as the Qur'an cannot be imitated, due mainly to the three essential aspects mentioned above.

At the end of each page, its verses become complete with a beautiful rhyme. Another sign of its miraculousness, this fine aspect is due to the fact that its longest verse (*Mudayana* [loan business]) provides the norm or standard length for pages, while *Surat al-Ikhlas* (Sincerity) and *Surat al-Kawthar* (Abundance) do the same for its lines.

their fingers in amazement and removed their most celebrated Seven Poems, which had been written in gold and hung on the Ka'ba's walls. Third, it forever silenced soothsayers and magicians by making them forget their knowledge of the Unseen and causing their jinn to be expelled from the heavens. Fourth, it saved those who knew some history and cosmology from myths and fabrications, and taught them the reality of past events and the illuminating facts of creation.

Thus these four groups, kneeling before the Qur'an in absolute astonishment and awe, became its students and never tried to challenge it.

A possible question: How do we know that nobody has disputed with it or that such a challenge is impossible?

Answer: If this were at all possible, someone would have tried it. Actually, the Qur'an's opponents needed such a challenge, for they felt that it endangered their religion and life, as well as their property. Thus they would have challenged the Qur'an if they could have done so. Many unbelievers and hypocrites were ready to advertise such a contest, just as they spread malicious propaganda against Islam.

If any challenge had been successful, it would have been recorded (with exaggeration). But all history books have come down to us, and none contain anything other than a few nonsensical lines of Musaylima al-Kadhdhab (the Liar), a self-proclaimed (and false) Prophet. They never dared to challenge it, although the Qur'an challenged them for 23 years in a way that provoked and annoyed them, as follows:

> Come on and produce a like of this Qur'an. Let an unlettered man, like Muhammad the Trustworthy, do so. If he cannot, let the most knowledgeable and well-versed in writing try. If he cannot, gather all of your learned and eloquent people and let them work together. Call upon your gods and goddesses. If you still cannot produce anything, use of all books of the highest eloquence, and let all unbelievers to come until Doomsday use your experiences in their attempt. If even then you cannot do so, try to produce the like of only 10 *suras*. If you cannot do this, make a composition from baseless stories and imaginative tales to match only the Qur'an's metrical verse and eloquence. If you cannot, produce only one chapter. If you cannot do even this, produce a short chapter, or else your

religion, lives, properties, and families will be at stake in this world and the Hereafter!

With these eight alternatives, the Qur'an has challenged and silenced all people and jinn for the last 14 centuries. Instead of preferring the easiest way (open challenge), the unbelievers living during the early days of Islam chose the hardest way (warfare) and so jeopardized their lives, properties, and families. If someone could have met even the easiest condition of this challenge, no people of wisdom, especially those living at the Prophet's time and the Qurayshi intellectual elite, would have been forced to choose warfare. In summary, as Jahiz put it, they had to resort to struggle by the sword since challenge by words was impossible.

Question: Some discerning scholars maintain that no Qur'anic *sura*, verse, sentence, or word can be disputed and that no one has ever done so successfully. This sounds exaggerated and hard to accept, as many human-produced words bear some resemblance to the Qur'an.

Answer: There are two opinions on its miraculousness. The prevailing opinion is that its eloquence and meaning's virtues are beyond human capacity. The other one says that one can challenge and compete with a *sura*, but that God Almighty prevents it as a miracle of Muhammad.

For example, if a Prophet told someone who could stand: "You will be unable to stand" and this came true, it would be considered a miracle of the Prophet. This school is known as Sarfa, which teaches that the All-Mighty prevents people and jinn from producing even a *sura*. If this were not true, they might challenge one *sura*. Thus scholars who maintain that not even a word of the Qur'an can be challenged are correct, for the All-Mighty prevents this on account of the Qur'an's miraculousness.

In the view of such scholars, however, there is a subtle point: All Qur'anic words and verses are interrelated. Sometimes a word is related to 10 other occurrences, thus bearing 10 relationships and providing 10 instances of eloquence. In my *Isharat al-I'jaz* (Signs of Miraculousness), a key to the Qur'an's interpretation, I show some examples drawn from the initial verses of *Surat al-Fatiha* and *Surat al-Baqara*.

For example, one can place a most important gem in the most proper place in the decorative pattern of a well-ornamented palace's wall only after knowing the whole design. Likewise, placing the eye's pupil in its correct location entails knowing all of the body's functions and complex organization as well as its relationship with the eye's function.

In just the same way, the foremost people of science and profound truth demonstrate numerous relationships between the Qur'an's words and each word's manifold relationships with other verses and expressions. Scholars of the mysteries of letters go even further, proving that each letter of the Qur'an has many inner meanings that, if explained fully, might cover pages.

Since the Qur'an is the Word of the Creator of everything, each word may function as the core or heart of an ideal body made of hidden meanings placed around it or as the seed of an ideal tree. Therefore, although some human-made words may be similar to those of the Qur'an, placing them properly by means of considering all relationships between [and among] the Qur'anic words calls for an all-comprehending knowledge.

THIRD POINT: God Almighty once inspired in my heart a brief reflection on the Qur'an's miraculous nature. I give its translation (from the original Arabic) below:

Glory be to God, Who Himself witnesses to His Oneness; Who has disclosed the qualities of His Grace, Majesty, and Perfection through the Qur'an; and Whose six sides are luminous and contain neither misgiving nor doubt. Supported by God's Throne of Sovereignty, from which it holds the light of Revelation, it leads to the happiness of the two worlds and aims at the light of Paradise and eternal bliss. Above it shines the seal of miraculousness, beneath it lie the pillars of proof and evidence, and inside it is pure guidance. It urges minds to seek its confirmation through such warnings as: Will they not comprehend and reflect? The spiritual pleasures it bestows upon the heart makes the conscience testify to its miraculousness. From which side or corner, then, could the arrows of doubt invade such a miraculous Qur'an?

The miraculous Qur'an includes the content of all books given to all Prophets as well as of all saints and monotheists regardless of path, temperament, and time. In other words, all people of heart and intellect mention the Qur'an's laws and fundamentals in their books in a way that shows their affirmation, and so are like roots of the "celestial tree of the Qur'an."

The Qur'an is truly a Revelation. The Majestic One Who revealed it proves this via the miracles He created at Muhammad's hands. Even the Qur'an's own miraculousness shows that it comes from God's Exalted Throne. Lastly, Prophet Muhammad's anxiety when the Revelation began, his half-conscious state when receiving it, and his unmatched sincere respect and devotion to the Qur'an all prove that it is Revelation, derived from past eternity,[295] and entrusted to the Prophet.

---

[295] Past eternity (*azel*) is not, as people imagine, just the starting-point of time and therefore essential for a thing's existence. In fact, past eternity is like a mirror that reflects the past, present, and future. Excluding themselves from time's passage, people tend to imagine a limit for past time that extends through a certain chain of things. They call this *past eternity*. Such a method of reasoning is neither right nor acceptable. The following subtle point may clarify matters. Imagine that you are holding a mirror. Everything reflected on the right represents the past, while everything reflected on the left represents the future. The mirror can reflect only one direction, since it cannot show both sides simultaneously while you are holding it. To do that, you have to rise so high above your original position that left and right become one, and there is no longer any difference between first and last, beginning or end. (Tr.)

The Qur'an is pure guidance, since its opposite (unbelief) is obviously misguidance. Of necessity, the Qur'an is the source of the light of belief, for the opposite of this light is darkness. The Qur'an is the spring of truths into which neither imagination nor superstition can find a way. The truthful world of Islam shaped by its Revelation, the well-founded law it presents, and the highest virtues that it manifests all testify to its complete truthfulness vis-à-vis the Unseen and the visible worlds.

The Qur'an shows the way and guides people to happiness in both worlds. Whoever doubts this should read it once and heed its words. Its perfect and life-giving fruits demonstrate that it is deeply rooted in truth and true vigor, for a fruit's vigor indicates a tree's life. Just look at how many perfect, vigorous, and luminous fruits—people of sainthood, purity, and profound learning—it yields in each century. Through the conviction and intuition coming from countless indications, the Qur'an is so esteemed and sought after by people, jinn, and angels that its recitation causes them to gather around it like moths.

In addition, all people of the profoundest knowledge agree that the Qur'an is confirmed and fortified by rational proofs. Such geniuses of philosophy as Ibn Sina (Avicenna) and Ibn Rushd (Averroës), and especially the most learned theologians, prove the truth of the Qur'an's fundamentals with their own methods of reasoning. Humanity's very nature, so long as it remains unspoiled, affirms the Qur'an's truth, for only its light can satisfy a person's conscience and place his or her heart placed at rest.

The Qur'an is an everlasting miracle that continually unfolds its miraculousness. It never fades or perishes like other miracles, nor does it age over time. The Qur'an's guidance is so inclusive and comprehensive that Archangel Gabriel and young children listen to it side by side, both deriving their lessons. Such a brilliant philosopher as Ibn Sina sits before it knee to knee with ordinary reciters to receive its teaching. Sometimes ordinary reciters, by virtue of their purity and strength of belief, derive more benefit than Ibn Sina.

The Qur'an's guidance provides such penetrating insight that the universe can be seen and comprehended like a book's pages. Like a watchmaker who opens and describes a watch down to its smallest part, the Qur'an expounds the universe with all of its spheres and particles. Above all, it states that "There is no deity but God" and declares His Oneness.

> O God, make the Qur'an our companion in the world and our confidant in the grave, our intercessor in the Hereafter and our light on the Sirat Bridge, a veil and protection against Hellfire, a friend in Paradise, and a guide and a leader to all goodness. O God, illumine our hearts and graves with the light of belief and the Qur'an, and brighten the evidence of the Qur'an for the sake of him to whom You sent it. Upon him and his Family be peace and blessings from the Compassionate and Solicitous One. Amen.

NINETEENTH SIGN: The previous signs proved that Muhammad is the Messenger of God Almighty. With his Messengership evident from thousands of decisive proofs, he is the brightest sign and most definite evidence of God's Oneness and [the existence of] eternal happiness. Here we give a brief description of this radiant sign, this truth-speaking evidence. Since he is the evidence via which the knowledge of God is acquired, we must recognize both the evidence and the way it acts as evidence.

God's Messenger, like every other being, is personally a proof of God's Existence and Unity. Moreover, he is the one who announced this truth in his own words and those of all other creatures. We now point out in 15 essentials how evident, upright, and truthful this proof is.

FIRST ESSENTIAL: The one who gives evidence of the universe's Maker in word, act, and conduct is truthful and confirmed by creation's truths, for all creatures, by being proofs of God's Unity, affirm the one who declares this Unity. Therefore all creation supports his cause. His cause also is truthful because his declaration, mainly comprising Divine Unity, signifies the pure blessing of absolute perfection and eternal happiness, and is in complete harmony with all universal truths' beauty and perfection. Given this, God's Messenger is an articulate and truthful proof of Divine Unity and eternal happiness, and all creation confirms his truthfulness.

SECOND ESSENTIAL: Since this truthful and certified proof has thousands of miracles excelling those of all other Prophets, as well as an eternal Sacred Law and a message embracing humanity and jinn, he is the head of all Prophets. Given this, he has the core of all their miracles as well as their unanimous confirmation. In other words, all other Prophets agree on the same belief, and their miracles support his honesty and truthfulness.

At the same time, he is the master and leader of all saints as well as of all people of purity and profound knowledge who have attained perfection through his teaching, guidance, and Sacred Law (the Shari'a). Thus he has the core of their wonders and unanimous affirmation, as well as the strength of their verified conclusions. Since he opened—and keeps open—the way they followed to reach the truth, all of their wonders, conclusions, and consensus on the same belief support his truthfulness. This proof of God's Unity, as shown in all previous signs, contains such certain, evident, and definite miracles and wonderful *irhasat* that, together with other evidences of his Prophethood, their affirmation cannot be disputed.

THIRD ESSENTIAL: This herald of God's Unity, who has so many evident miracles, and this bearer of the good tidings of eternal happiness has such sublime virtues in his blessed being, such exalted qualities in his Messengership, and such precious merits in the religion and Sacred Law that he preached that even his bitterest enemies admitted them.

Since he combines the most praiseworthy virtues in his personality, function, and religion, he is the embodiment, master, and representative of all perfections and high, laudable virtues found in creation. This perfect state that he reached in his being, task, and religion is such a strong proof and support for his honesty and truthfulness that it cannot be shaken.

Fourth essential: This herald of God's Oneness and eternal happiness, the source of all perfections and teacher of the highest morality, speaks only what is revealed and what he is taught to speak by his Eternal Master. This is because, as partly explained in previous signs, the universe's Creator provided him with thousands of miracles to prove his Prophethood and to show that he speaks on His behalf and communicates His message. Second, the Qur'an's 40 miraculous aspects show that the Prophet is the All-Mighty's interpreter.

Third, his perfect sincerity, righteousness, earnestness, trustworthiness, and all other acts and states show that he speaks only on his Creator's behalf. Fourth, all people of truth who have listened to him affirm, through profound study and inspired discovery, and believe with the certainty of true knowledge that he does not speak on his own authority; rather, the universe's Creator teaches him and makes him speak what He has taught him. The evidence explained so far in these essentials, when joined together, is a very strong support for his honesty and truthfulness.

FIFTH ESSENTIAL: This interpreter of God's eternal Word sees spirits, converses with angels, and guides humanity and jinn alike. He teaches humanity and jinn, inhabitants of the incorporeal abode, and angels, showing that he has access to and relationships with realms beyond these abodes. The above-mentioned miracles and his very life prove this. Thus his reports of the Unseen do not resemble those of soothsayers. No person, jinn, spirit, or angel (except for Gabriel) has any say in his reports. And there are many times when even Gabriel falls behind him.

SIXTH ESSENTIAL: This master of angels, humanity, and jinn is the Tree of Creation's most perfect and most radiant fruit, the embodiment of His compassion, the reflection of the Lord's love, the most brilliant proof of the All-Mighty, the brightest light of truth, the key to the universe's hidden truths, the discloser of creation's mystery, the expounder of creation's Divine purpose, the proclaimer of God's kingship, the describer of His beautiful art, and, by virtue of his comprehensive faculties, the most excellent pattern of all of creation's perfections.

Such character qualities, together with his spiritual personality, clearly demonstrate that he is the ultimate cause for the universe's creation or, in other words, that the Creator created the universe on his pattern. It even can be argued that if God had not created him, He would not have created the universe. Certainly, the Qur'anic truths and the light of belief that he brought to humanity and jinn, along with the most exalted virtues and illustrious perfections observed in his being, are the evident proofs of this argument.

SEVENTH ESSENTIAL: This "proof of the Truth" (*al-Haqq*) and "light of the truth" offers such a religion and Sacred Law that it contains all principles for securing happiness in both worlds. They perfectly expound the universe's truths and functions, as well the Creator of the universe's

Names and Attributes. Islam and its Sacred Law are so perfect and comprehensive, and describe the universe and its Creator in such a way, that whoever reflects on Islam realizes that it is the declaration of the One Who made this beautiful universe and that it describes the universe and its Maker.

Like a spectacular palace revealing its architect's skill, and the book written by the architect so that others may know it better, the religion and Sacred Law preached by Prophet Muhammad demonstrate, through their comprehensiveness, sublimity, and truth, that they are designed by the same Being Who created and continues to manage the universe. Indeed, the universe's perfect order calls for that most beautiful system of Islam as its expression in the Realm of Conscious Beings.

EIGHTH ESSENTIAL: Distinguished with these qualities and supported by the most unshakable proofs, Prophet Muhammad proclaims his message to humanity and jinn, in the name of the Unseen, to all people regardless of time and place. And, his voice is so strong that all of them will hear him, just as we do.

Ninth essential: His speech is so effective and penetrating that people in all times listen to him, and his voice is echoed in every century.

Tenth essential: His manner reveals that he sees and communicates what he sees, for even at the most perilous times he speaks with utmost conviction and assurance and challenges the world.

Eleventh essential: He calls with such vigor and from the depths of his heart that half of the world and one-fifth of humanity has submitted to the Qur'an obediently.

Twelfth essential: He invites so earnestly, and guides and trains so radically, that he leaves his principles as permanent, unerasable marks throughout all times and places.

Thirteenth essential: His trust and confidence in the soundness of the commands that he preaches are so great that he would never retract or regret one of them, even if the whole world united against him. Every instance of his life is a witness to this.

Fourteenth essential: He calls with such conviction and certainty that he is indebted to no one and shows no anxiety, regardless of circumstances. With utmost sincerity and honesty, and without hesitation, he is the first to accept and practice what he communicates to others. His piety and contentment, as well as his disdain for the world's transient allurements, prove this fact that is known to friends and foes alike.

FIFTEENTH ESSENTIAL: He is the first and foremost in obeying Islam, worshipping his Creator, and observing the religious prohibitions. This proves that he is the King of eternity's envoy, announcer, and most sincere servant, as well as the interpreter of His Eternal Word.

From these 15 essentials, we conclude that this person, distinguished with the qualities mentioned, devoted his life to one principle and declared it continuously: "There is no deity but God," and thus proclaimed God's absolute Oneness.

> O God, bestow on him and his Family peace and blessings to the number of his community's good deeds. Glory be to You, we have no knowledge save what You have taught us. You are the All-Knowing, the All-Wise.

APPENDIX 1

Further remarks about the Prophet's greatness

In the Name of God,
the Merciful, the Compassionate.

FIRST DROPLET: Three great and universal things make our Lord known to us: the Book of the Universe (explained elsewhere), the Seal of the Prophets (the Book of the Universe's supreme sign), and the Qur'an. Now we must recognize and listen to the Seal of the Prophets, that articulate proof and announcer of God with all His Names and Attributes, His Existence and Unity.

Look at that illustrious proof's universal personality: Earth's surface is his mosque, Makka is his *mihrab* (prayer niche), and Madina is his pulpit. Our Prophet is the leader of all believers, preacher to all humanity, chief of all Prophets, lord of all saints, and leader in the remembrance of God of a circle comprising all Prophets and saints. With all Prophets as its roots and all saints as its ever-fresh fruits, he is a radiant tree. All Prophets, with the support of their miracles, and all saints, relying on their wonders, confirm and corroborate his claim that "There is no deity but God." All illustrious reciters of God's Names lined up in the past and future repeat these words in unison, as if to say: "You speak the truth, and what you say is right!" What illusion can dispute an argument confirmed by such countless endorsements?

SECOND DROPLET: Just as the consensus and unanimity of all Prophets and saints affirm this radiant proof of Divine Unity, hundreds of signs in the revealed Scriptures (e.g., the Torah and the Gospels), thousands of indications of his Prophethood that appeared prior to his mission, famous reports of voices from the Unseen, soothsayers' unanimous testimony, thousands of miracles, and the justice and truth of his Shari'a all confirm and corroborate him.

Similarly, his laudable virtues' perfection, his complete confidence in his mission, his most excellent qualities in relation to its fulfillment, and his extraordinary awe of God, worship, serenity, and firmness—all show the strength of his belief. In addition, his total certainty and complete steadfastness clearly show his claim's undeniable truth.

THIRD DROPLET: In our imagination, let's go to Arabia during the Age of Bliss and visit him while he is performing his mission. Look! We see a person distinguished by his character's excellence and form's beauty. Holding a miraculous book and speaking truthfully, he delivers an eternal sermon to humanity, jinn, angels—indeed to all beings. He solves and expounds the mystery of the world's creation, discovers and solves the universe's intricate mystery, and gives convincing and satisfying answers to questions asked constantly by all beings: Who am I? What is my life's purpose? Where did I come from? Were am I going? What is my final destination?

FOURTH DROPLET: Behold! He spreads such a light of truth that, if you look at the universe without the light of his guidance, you see it as a place of mourning, of beings that are alien or even hostile to each another, of inanimate beings that are ghastly corpses, and of living creatures that are orphans weeping under the blows of death and separation. But the light he spreads transforms that place of universal mourning into a place of invocation where God's Names and praises are recited in joy and ecstasy. Those alien, hostile beings are friends, brothers, and sisters. Dumb, inanimate creatures take the form of familiar, obedient officials and docile servants. Weeping, complaining orphans either recite God's Names and praises or offer thanks for being discharged from their duties.

FIFTH DROPLET: Again, through this light, the universe's motions, variations, changes, and transformations are no longer considered meaningless and futile playthings of chance, but appear in their true form and function: missives of the universe's Master, a page inscribed with the signs of creation, a mirror reflecting God's Names. The world itself is shown to be a book of the Eternally-Besought-of-All's wisdom. Without this light, our boundless weakness, helplessness, poverty, and neediness cause us to fall lower than animals. And then our intellect makes us even more wretched by conveying grief, sorrow, and anxiety to us.

But when this light illumines us, we rise above all animals and creatures, and our poverty and helplessness become means of infinite wealth and power by our dependence on God. We ascend to the level of being a beloved monarch through entreaty, and through lamenting we become a vicegerent of Earth. In other words, only this light prevents the universe, humanity, and all things from being reduced to nothingness. Such a person is necessary in such a wondrous universe, for without him there would be no need for the universe and all the worlds to exist.

SIXTH DROPLET: This being announces and brings good tidings of eternal happiness. He unveils and proclaims God's infinite Mercy, observes and heralds the beauties of the Realm of the Lord's Sovereignty, and discloses and displays the Divine Names' treasures. If you observe him as a devoted worshipper of God, you will see him to be a model of love and an embodiment of mercy, as well as the pride of humanity and the Tree of Creations' most illustrious fruit. If you observe him as a Messenger, you will see him to be a proof of God, a lamp of truth, a sun of guidance, and the means of happiness.

Look! His light has lit up from East to West like dazzling lightning, and half of the globe and one-fifth of humanity have accepted his guidance and preserved it like their lives. So why should our evil-commanding selves and satans not accept "There is no deity but God," the essence of his mission?

SEVENTH DROPLET: Consider how he eradicated his people's deep attachment to evil and savage customs and immoral qualities; equipped and adorned his desperate, wild, and unyielding people with all praiseworthy virtues; and made them the world's teachers and masters, especially to the "civilized" nations. His domination was not outward; rather, he conquered and subjugated their minds, spirits, hearts, and souls. He became the beloved of hearts, teacher of minds, trainer of souls, and ruler of spirits.

EIGHTH DROPLET: A small habit like smoking can be removed permanently from a small community only by a powerful ruler and with great effort. But see how this man quickly removed numerous ingrained habits from large obsessed communities with little outward power and little effort, and replaced them with exalted qualities that became inherent in their being. He did many more such miraculous things. To those who refuse to see the testimony of that blessed time, we challenge them with Arabia's present-day reality. Let them go there with hundreds of philosophers, sociologists, and psychologists for a century and see if they can achieve even one-hundredth of what the Prophet achieved in a year.

NINTH DROPLET: An unimportant person cannot lie to a group of people about something insignificant without betraying himself or herself via anxiety or unease. Yet this person, while undertaking a tremendous task in the name of Messengership and needing protection against his enemies, easily speaks about great causes before large congregations without any anxiety or hesitation.

Furthermore, no contradictions can be found in what he proclaims with such pure sincerity and great seriousness. In addition, he does so in such an intense, elevated manner that he irritates his enemies. How could there have been any deception? What he speaks is nothing but Revelation revealed. The truth cannot be deceptive, and one who sees it cannot be deceived. His path, which is pure truth, contains no deception.

TENTH DROPLET: Consider the curiosity-arousing, attractive, necessary, and awesome truths that he shows and the matters that he proves. Everyone is curious. Suppose someone said: "If you give half of your property, someone will come from Mars or Jupiter to tell you about them, as well as your future and what will happen to you." If you have any curiosity at all, you will do as requested. But this person talks of other things: of a Monarch in whose realm the moon flies round a moth (Earth) like a fly, and the moth flutters round a lamp (the sun), which is just one of thousands of lamps in one of the Monarch's countless guesthouses. Also, he speaks truly of so wondrous a world and predicts such a revolution that it would not be strange if Earth was a bomb and exploded. Listen to the *suras* he recites, which begin with:

> When the sun is folded up. (81:1)
>
> When the sky is cleft asunder. (82:1)
>
> (The day) of Noise and Clamor. (101:1)

He speaks so truly of such a future that, in relation to it, the future in this world is like a trifling mirage. He tells us so solemnly of such happiness that all worldly happiness is like a flash of lightning in comparison to an eternal sun.

ELEVENTH DROPLET: Such wonders await us under the universe's apparent veil. We need a wonderful and miracle-working person to communicate and explain these wonders to us. His conduct proves that he has seen—and sees—them, and he tells us what he sees. He teaches us what the One God of those heavens and Earth,

Who nourishes us with His bounties, wants of us and how we can please Him. While we should drop everything in order to run to and then heed this person who instructs us in these and many other necessary and curiosity-arousing things, most people are so deaf and blind—even mad—that they do not see, hear, or understand this truth.

TWELFTH DROPLET: As well as being an articulate proof and truthful evidence of the Oneness of the Creator of all beings, he is a decisive proof and clear evidence of the Resurrection and eternal happiness. Given that he is the cause for gaining eternal happiness through his guidance, he is the cause of its existence and the means of its creation through his prayers and supplications.

See! While supplicating during this supreme prayer, it is as if Arabia—even Earth—prays through his sublime presence and makes its petition. He entreats amid so vast a congregation that it is as if all illustrious people of perfection from Adam until the end of time are following him and saying "Amen" to his supplications. He implores on behalf of so universal a need that the inhabitants of Earth and the heavens, indeed all beings, join in his prayer, saying: "Yes, O Master, grant that to us, for we also desire it." He supplicates so needily and sorrowfully, in such a loving, longing, and entreating fashion, that he brings the universe to tears and causes it to join in his prayer.

And see! The goal and purpose for which he prays elevates humanity and the world—all creation—from the lowest ranks of humiliation, worthlessness, and uselessness to the highest ranks of having value, permanence, and sublime duties. He supplicates and petitions in a manner so elevated and help-seeking, so sweet and mercy-imploring, that it is as if he causes all beings and the heavens and the Divine Throne of Grace to hear. And then, bringing them to ecstasy, he causes them to exclaim: "Amen, O God, Amen!"

He begs his needs from so Powerful a Being, All-Hearing and All-Generous, from so All-Knowing a Being, All-Seeing and All-Merciful, that that Being sees the most hidden being's secret need, hears and accepts its entreaties, and has mercy on it. He meets its need, even though this being asks for it through the tongue of its disposition, and gives it in such a wise, seeing, and compassionate form that it leaves no doubt that only an All-Hearing and All-Seeing One, One Most Generous and Most Merciful, can do so.

THIRTEENTH DROPLET: What does he want, this pride of humanity, this unique being and glory of all beings, who stands for prayer with all eminent people behind him and with hands upraised? He is seeking eternal happiness, eternal life, a meeting with God, and Paradise. He wants all of these through the Divine Names, which display their beauty and operations in the mirrors of beings. Even one of his prayers, were it not for such innumerable causes as Mercy, Grace, Wisdom, and Justice fulfilling that request, would be enough to build Paradise, which is as easy for Divine Power as creating spring. Just as his Messengership opened this place of trial, his worship and servitude to God opened a way to the next world.

I wonder how the universe's perfect order, which causes wise and reflective people to say that no "new" universe could be more original and wonderful, as well as the flawless beauty of His Mercy's art and His Mastership's matchless beauty, could be at all consonant with ugliness, mercilessness, and disorder. How could He refuse the most important and necessary desires while satisfying the most insignificant wishes. It is impossible!

So, my imaginary friend, let's return. Even if we stayed for 100 years we could not comprehend fully even one-hundredth of his marvelous and remarkable acts. We would never tire of observing him. During our return, we will look at each century to see how each has bloomed fully through the flow of light received from that Sun of Guidance, and how it yielded thousands of such illustrious fruits as Abu Hanifa, Shafi'i, Bayazid al-Bistami, 'Abd al-Qadir al-Jilani, Shah Naqshband, Imam Ghazzali, and Imam Rabbani.

Postponing the details of our observations, we should invoke blessings on that worker of miracles and bringer of guidance that refer to some of his certain miracles:

> Upon him—our master Muhammad—to whom the All-Compassionate and All-Merciful One sent the Wise Criterion of Truth (the Qur'an) from the Mighty Throne, be peace and blessings equaling the number of his community's good deeds. Upon him whose Messengership was foretold by the Torah, Gospels, and Psalms; whose Prophethood was pre-

dicted by wondrous events prior to his Prophethood, and by the voices of jinn, saints of humanity, and soothsayers; and at whose gesture the moon split, may there be peace and blessings equaling the number of his community's breaths.

Upon him at whose beckoning trees came; by whose prayer rain fell; whom the cloud shaded from the heat; who made one dish of food satisfy hundreds of people; from whose fingers water flowed like the Spring of Kawthar; to whom God caused the lizard, the gazelle, the wolf, the camel, the mountain, the rock, the pole, and the clod of earth to speak; the one who made the Ascension (Mi'raj) and whose eye did not waver, may there be peace and blessings equaling the number of letters (in the Qur'an) formed in the words represented, with the All-Compassionate's permission, in the mirrors of the airwaves when all reciters of the Qur'an, from the beginning of Revelation until the end of time, recite its words. Forgive us and have mercy upon us, O God, for the sake of each of those blessings. Amen.

FOURTEENTH DROPLET: The Qur'an, the treasury of miracles and itself a supreme miracle, proves his Prophethood and God's Oneness so decisively that no further proof is needed. We now define this miracle and refer to one or two flashes of its miraculousness that have been criticized.

The Qur'an, which makes our Master known to us, is an eternal translator of the great Book of the Universe; the discloser of the Divine Names' treasures hidden in the pages of Earth and the heavens; the key to the truths lying beneath the lines of events; the treasury of the All-Compassionate's favors; the eternal addresses coming from the Unseen world beyond this visible world's veil; the sun of Islam's spiritual and intellectual world; the foundation, plan, and map of the Hereafter's worlds; the expounder, lucid interpreter, articulate proof, and clear translator of the Divine Essence, Attributes, and acts; humanity's educator, trainer, guide, and leader; and true wisdom. It is a book of wisdom and law, prayer and worship, command and summons, invocation and knowledge of God; a book that contains books for all of humanity's spiritual needs, like a sacred library offering books from which all saints, eminently truthful people, and all purified and discerning scholars derive their particular ways.

Consider the flash of miraculousness in its reiterations, which are imagined to be a fault. Yet such reiteration is desirable, for the Qur'an is a book of invocation, prayer, and summons. In this context, reiteration is a most necessary and beautiful eloquence, for invoking God requires that the Qur'an be able to impress and enlighten hearts. Through repetition, prayer acquires and gives strength and becomes ingrained in hearts. Commands and summons need restatement to be confirmed and enforced.

Moreover, not everyone can read the whole Qur'an any time he or she wants, but usually can read one *sura*. Thus the Qur'an reiterates its most important purposes in most of the longer *suras*, each of which thereby becomes like a small Qur'an. Such purposes and themes as Divine Unity, Resurrection, and the story of Moses are repeated so that no one is deprived of their benefits.

Furthermore, spiritual tastes and needs vary, just like bodily tastes and needs. Humanity is in need of some at every breath. Just like the body needs air, the spirit needs the particle *Hu–Huwa* (He–God). It needs others every hour, like

Bismillah (In the Name of God). Reiteration therefore arises from recurring need, and to point out those needs, make them deeply felt, and awaken people to the need to satisfy them.

Also the Qur'an is the founder and basis of the perfect religion (Islam) and the foundation of its world. It came to change humanity's social life and answer people's recurring questions. Repetition is necessary for a founder to affirm, and reiteration is necessary to emphasize. Establishing something new requires confirmation and strengthening, and therefore repetition.

The Qur'an speaks of such important matters and subtle truths that reiteration is necessary in different contexts to impress them on people's minds and hearts. Actually, such repetition is only apparent, for in reality each word has manifold meanings, numerous benefits, and many aspects and levels. The words or verses always occur in a different place, way, context, and for a different meaning, purpose, and benefit. Certain cosmological matters are mentioned in a concise, allusive way. Doing so is not a fault, as some unbelievers and atheists assert, but rather a flash of miraculousness, for the Qur'an came to guide humanity.

QUESTION: Why does the Qur'an not speak of beings in the same way as science and materialistic or naturalistic philosophy? It mentions some matters very briefly and others in an apparently simple and superficial way that is easy for ordinary people to understand.

ANSWER: Science and materialistic philosophy have strayed from the path of truth. The Qur'an is not a science book, and so does not need to dwell on cosmological matters. It mentions certain facts of creation to make known the Divine Essence, Attributes, and Names by explaining the meaning of the Book of the Universe so that its Creator may be known. Therefore it considers creation for the sake of gaining knowledge of its Creator. Science, on the other hand, considers creation for its own sake and addresses scientists in particular.

As the Qur'an addresses all people, most of whom are ordinary, and uses creation as evidence and proof to guide humanity, the presented evidence should be clear and obvious to ensure easy understanding. In addition, guidance requires that unimportant things only be touched on and that subtle points be explained through parables. To avoid leading people into error, it should not change things considered obvious in a way that confuses or even harms its audience.

For example, the Qur'an calls the sun a *moving lamp* because it is the "mainstay" of the universe's order and its system's center, and order and system are two means of acquiring knowledge of the Creator. When it says: *And the sun runs its course* (36:38), it suggests Divine Power's well-ordered disposition in the revolutions of seasons, and day and night, and so implies the Maker's majesty. Thus the reality of this "running" does not harm the intended meaning—the observed order woven into the universe's structure.

The Qur'an also says: *And He made the sun as a lamp* (71:16). Depicting the sun as a lamp reminds us that the world resembles a palace containing the decorations, provisions, and other necessities prepared for humanity and all living creatures. The sun functions as a lamp to illuminate it, implying the Creator's mercy and bounty.

Now consider how science and materialistic philosophy describe the sun: "The sun is an enormous mass of burning gases. It causes the planets, which have been flung off from it, to revolve around it. It is of such-and-such size, and has such-

and-such qualities." It gives no perfection of knowledge to the spirit, but only a terrible dread and bewilderment. It does not approach the matter as the Qur'an does.

From this comparison, judge the value of the scientific and philosophical way of thinking, the former of which is outwardly splendid but inwardly hollow. So do not be fooled by the outward worth of scientific descriptions and become disrespectful toward the Qur'an's most miraculous style.

> O God, make the Qur'an a cure for all sickness for us, a companion to us in life and after death, a friend in the world, a confidant in the grave, an intercessor on the Day of Judgment, a light on the (Bridge of) Sirat, a veil and a screen from Hellfire, a friend in Paradise, and a guide and a leader to all good deeds. By Your grace, munificence, beneficence, and mercy, O Most Generous of the generous and Most Merciful of the merciful. Amen.
>
> O God, bestow blessings and peace on him to whom You sent the Qur'an, the Criterion of Truth and Falsehood, and on all members of his Family and his Companions. Amen.

APPENDIX 2

The miracle of splitting the moon

In the name of God,
the Merciful, the Compassionate.

> The Hour has approached, and the moon split. But whenever they see a sign, they turn away, saying: "This is evidently part of (his) magic." (54:1-2)

QUESTION: Materialist philosophers and their imitators, who want to deny this bright miracle of Prophet Muhammad, say: "If the event really happened, it would have been known all over the world and related in all historical documents."

ANSWER: This miracle occurred before a group of people to convince them of his Prophethood. It happened momentarily when people were sleeping; such obstacles as mist, clouds, and time differences prevented others from seeing it; and science and civilization were not yet advanced or widespread. Thus observing the sky was quite limited. Last but not least, there is no reason why it should have been seen worldwide. To remove such clouds of delusion, consider the following five points:

FIRST POINT: The stubbornness of Muhammad's unbelieving contemporaries is well-known and recorded. When the Qur'an proclaimed this incident in *the moon split,* not one unbeliever dared contradict it. If they had not seen this event, they would have used this verse as a pretext to attack the Prophet more formidably.

But nothing in the biographies of the Prophet or history books suggest they denied it. Their reaction was: *This is evidently part of his magic,* and added that if caravans in other places had seen it, it had truly happened; otherwise, the Prophet had bewitched them. When caravans arriving the following morning from Yemen and other places announced that they had seen this miracle, the unbelievers replied: "The magic of Abu Talib's orphan has affected even the heavens!"

SECOND POINT: The majority of the foremost scholars of meticulous research, such as Sa'd al-Din al-Taftazani, concluded that, like the earlier-mentioned miracles of water flowing from the Prophet's fingers and the audible grieving of the wooden pole against which the Prophet used to lean while delivering sermons, when it was separated from him following the construction of a pulpit, the splitting of the moon is *mutawatir*. This means that it has been transmitted down the generations by one truthful group after another, and that the transmitters form such a vast community that they are unable to agree on a lie. It is as certain as Haley's comet, which appeared 1,000 years ago, or the existence of an island we have not seen.

Therefore it is unreasonable to foster baseless doubts about such certain, witnessed matters. In fact, it is enough for their acceptability that they are not impossible. Splitting the moon is just as possible as splitting a mountain by a volcanic eruption.

THIRD POINT: Prophets work miracles to prove their Prophethood and to convince deniers, not to compel belief. Thus every miracle is shown to convince those who heard the claim of Prophethood. If they forced everyone to see or believe in them, the All-Wise's Wisdom, the Divine purpose for creating us with free will and sending religion, which entails that the ground be prepared for the mind's willing acceptance, would be violated.

Thus if the All-Wise Creator had left the moon split for several hours so that everyone could see it and record it in their historical records, it would have been only another astronomical event instead of an event unique to his Messengership or an evidence of his Prophethood. If everyone had been compelled to believe, free will would be annulled and Abu Jahl's coal-like spirit would be equal to Abu Bakr's diamond-like spirit. Thus the purpose of creating humanity with a special function and responsibility, as well as the purpose for sending revelation, would be negated. That is why this miracle was not shown worldwide so that it could be recorded.

FOURTH POINT: Some argue that if this event really occurred, Chinese, Japanese, and Native American historical accounts would mention it.[296] But how could they have seen it for, along with other obstacles, it was barely sunset in such European countries as Spain, France, and England (all enveloped in mists of ignorance), daytime in America, and morning in China and Japan.

---

[296] Some books also state that the moon fell to Earth after it split into two parts. Truthful scholars reject this, for it was added by a hypocrite who intended to reduce this evident miracle's value to nothing.

FIFTH POINT: This miracle is not an ordinary incident that happened due to particular causes or randomly so that it should be criticized based on the law of cause and effect. Rather, the All-Wise Creator of the sun and the moon made it an extraordinary event to confirm His Messenger's Prophethood and support his claim. Thus it was shown as a convincing proof to certain people and specified by Divine Wisdom, for the nature of Divine guidance and human responsibility as well as the reason for raising a Messenger required this. If it had been seen by those who were not intended to see it and who had not yet heard of his Prophethood, and if it had occurred according to the law of cause and effect, it would have been an ordinary astronomical event instead of a miracle specific to and connected with his Messengership.

In conclusion, these arguments are enough for any mind to be convinced of the possibility that this miracle occurred. Out of many evidences of its occurrence, we shall mention only six, as these six have the strength of a six-fold consensus:

- The Companions, all people of justice and truthfulness, agree that it took place.

- All exacting Qur'anic interpreters agree that the moon split indicates that a gesture of Muhammad's fingers caused this event.

- All truthful Traditionists narrated this incident through various authentic channels of transmission.

- All people of truth, sainthood, inspiration, and spiritual discovery testify that this event took place.

- All foremost theologians and learned scholars confirm this event, despite their other differences of opinions.

- Muhammad's community, which an authentic Prophetic Tradition states can never agree on an error, accepts its occurrence.

These six evidences clearly prove the splitting of the moon. Thus we have established this miracle's reality by refuting objections to its possibility. In a few concluding sentences, we will speak in the name of the truth and for the sake of belief.

The Seal of the Prophets, the luminous moon of the heaven of Messengership, proved his sainthood through his Ascension. His sainthood's greatest miracle, achieved through the quality of his worship, elevated him to the status of God's beloved. By making Muhammad travel through the heavens, God showed its dwellers and those of the highest realms that he is their superior and His beloved.

By allowing a man's gesture to split the moon, which is set in the sky and bound to Earth, people saw another great evidence of his Messengership. Thus the Prophet flew to the summit of perfections on the two brilliant wings of Messengership and sainthood (like the moon's two bright halves), ascended to *two bows' length* (the highest rank and nearest station to God), and became the cause of pride for all inhabitants of the heavens and Earth.

> Upon him and his Family be blessings and peace such as to fill Earth and the heavens. Glory be unto You. We have no knowledge save what You have taught us. You are the All-Knowing, All-Wise.
>
> O God, for the sake of him by a gesture of whom the moon split, make my heart and the hearts of the *Risale-i Nur's* students as devoted and loyal to the "sun" of the Qur'an as the moon is to the sun. Amen.

APPENDIX 3

Why only Prophet Muhammad was honored with the Ascension

The reason for this lies in his essential perfection and the nature of his Prophethood. First of all, Prophet Muhammad was expected for a long time, and his coming was promised through many signs. Given this, there are numerous proofs of his Prophethood. Although elaborated in previous chapters, we briefly list the signs showing his perfection and the proofs of his Prophethood to show that he was the most worthy to make the Ascension.

FIRST: Despite the great corruption in the Torah, Gospels, and Psalms, Husain al-Jisri's *Risala al-Hamidiya* presents 110 signs found in them that indicate Muhammad's Prophethood.

SECOND: History also records the words of many pre-Islamic soothsayers, such Shiq and Satih, who foretold his Prophethood and that he was the Last Prophet.

THIRD: Many extraordinary events (*irhasat*) before his Prophethood foretold the coming of a

Prophet. For example, on the night he was born, the Ka'ba's idols toppled over and the pinnacles of the famous palace of the Persian ruler Chosroes broke.

FOURTH: Muhammad was distinguished with approximately 1,000 miracles, all of which have been related by historians and biographers. To cite only a few examples, he satisfied an army's thirst with water flowing from his fingers and split the moon (54:1), and the dry wooden pole against which he leaned while preaching in the mosque moaned like a camel in front of many people when it was separated from him.

FIFTH: Friend and foe agree that all good qualities were found in him to the highest degree, and that, as shown by his conduct, all attributes and character of the highest excellence were apparent in the way he performed his mission. In accordance with Islam's moral principles, praiseworthy virtues of the highest order are found in the law that he brought.

SIXTH: Wisdom requires that Divinity be shown because of Its perfections. Prophet Muhammad manifested God's Divinity at the highest level and in the most brilliant fashion through the most perfect and comprehensive way of worship contained in the religion that he brought. Due to the wisdom in the universe's creation, the Creator of the world wills to display His most perfect Beauty and Grace through the most appropriate means. Clearly, Prophet Muhammad showed and described His Beauty and Grace in the most perfect fashion.

The Maker of the world wills to show and draw attentive gazes to His perfect art of infinite Beauty; the Prophet proclaimed that art with the clearest voice. In response to the Lord of the worlds' will to proclaim His Oneness in the realms of multiplicity, Muhammad announced His Unity with all of Its aspects most perfectly.

Due to His Wisdom, the Owner of the world wills to see and show His infinite essential Beauty and Grace, with all of their manifestations, in the mirrors of all beings; Muhammad reflected them in the most brilliant fashion and made others love them. In response to the will of the Builder of the palace of the world to describe His perfections by showing His unseen treasuries of priceless gems, Muhammad displayed and described them most perfectly.

The Maker of the universe has decorated the universe with the most beautiful and exquisite embellishments, and has included therein His conscious creatures so that they may travel to receive enjoyment and reflect. Due to His Wisdom, He wills to communicate the meaning and value expressed by the works of His art to people who observe and reflect. Muhammad guided humanity, jinn, and angels in the most comprehensive way, in this respect, through the Qur'an.

The All-Wise Ruler of the universe wills to use an envoy to reveal the purpose of the changes and transformations in existence, as well as to answer three perplexing questions asked by all conscious beings: Where do we come from? Where are we going? What are we? Through the Qur'an's truths, Muhammad revealed this purpose and the answers in the clearest and most perfect way.

The Maker of this world wills to make Himself known to conscious beings through His exquisite works and to be loved by them through the precious bounties He bestows on them. Thus He wills to communicate to them, via an envoy, what He wants them to do and how they may obtain His approval in return for those bounties. By means of the Qur'an, Muhammad related the things that please God in the most exalted and perfect way.

The Lord of the worlds has endowed humanity, the Tree of Creation's fruit, with a comprehensive disposition that can encompass the universe, and with a corresponding ability—and even need—to perform a universal worship. But humanity, due to its feelings, inclines to the world and its attractions. So God wills to turn humanity's attention from worldly multiplicity to Divine Unity, from transience to eternity, through a guide. In response to this will and via the Qur'an, Muhammad guided humanity to this goal in the most desirable fashion and performed the duty of Messengership in the most perfect way.

Thus creation's most superior members are living beings, the most superior living beings are conscious beings, the most superior conscious beings are true human beings, and that true human being who carried out all duties mentioned, in the most perfect and comprehensive way, would rise through an all-embracing Ascension to *the nearness of two bowstrings* (the station nearest to God), knock at the door of eternal happiness, and open the treasury of Mercy.

Thus the most superior members of creation are living beings, the most superior living beings are conscious beings, the most superior conscious beings are true human beings, and the true human being who carried out all of the duties mentioned in the most perfect and comprehensive way naturally would rise through an all-embracing Ascension to *the nearness of two bows' length*, the station nearest to God, to knock at the door of eternal happiness, open Mercy's treasury, and witness belief's unseen truths directly.

SEVENTH: Moreover, everything displays the most pleasing instances of beauty and utmost degree of adornment, thereby demonstrating that their Maker wills to make things beautiful and adorn them. In turn, this shows that the Maker has a strong inclination and sacred love toward His art. Therefore the person with the most comprehensive disposition to display this art's wonders in himself; one who knows them, makes them known, and thus makes himself lovable; and who deeply appreciates the beauties manifested in other beings in full appreciation of their coming from the Maker will be the most beloved in the Maker's sight, as He greatly loves His art.

This same being, in full awareness of the exquisite qualities adorning all beings and of the perfections illuminating them, makes the heavens echo: "Glory be to God! What wonders God has willed" and "All these are from God! God is the greatest!" This same being causes the universe to reverberate with the sounds of the Qur'an, and enraptures the land and the sea with his appreciative reflections and glorification as well as with his proclamation and demonstration of Divine Unity.

Such a being, according to the principle of "The cause is like the doer," receives a reward equivalent to his community's good deeds. His spiritual perfections draw strength from the blessings invoked upon him by his community, and the duties he performed during his Messengership cause him to receive an immaterial recompense and infinite emanations of Divine Mercy and Love. Given this, the result of pure truth and absolute wisdom is that this being should advance by means of Ascension as far as Paradise, *Sidrat al-Muntaha*—the lote tree, contingency's farthest limit—the Divine Throne, and to the *nearness of two bows' length*.

***

Appendix 4

About knowing the Prophet

Someone begins an intellectual journey to find and know the universe's Creator. After traveling in the realms of creatures, he[297] says to himself: "As I am seeking this universe's Creator and Owner amidst these creatures, first I should visit Muhammad and seek from him the answer to my quest." Using his imagination, he enters the Pro-

---

[297] The Qur'an declares: *I shall not allow to go to waste the deed of any one of you, whether male or female. You are one from the other* (3:195). It is clear that Islam does not discriminate between men and women in religious responsibility. Each gender shares most of the responsibilities, but each one has certain responsibilities that are particular to it. The Qur'an usually uses the masculine form of address, for this is one of Arabic's characteristics. In almost every language, the masculine form is used for a group comprising both men and women, like the English word *mankind*, which includes both men and women. So, *brotherhood* also includes sisterhood, and, since the believers comprise both male and female believers, the believers are bothers and sisters. However, in order to maintain the original text and avoid repetition, usually we do not mention the feminine forms in translation. (Tr.)

phet's blessed age and sees that it really was an era of happiness, for even his enemies confirmed him as the most blessed of creation, the greatest and most accomplished commander, the most celebrated ruler, the most exalted in speech, and the most brilliant in intellect. He has enlightened 14 centuries with his virtues and the Qur'an.

After investigating, the traveler realizes how the Prophet quickly transformed his primitive and illiterate people into the world's masters and teachers via the light that he brought. He finds numerous decisive proofs, in his character and mission, of the Creator's Existence and Oneness. Here we briefly point out nine of the most general ones, as follows:

FIRST: The Prophet possessed all laudable virtues and excellent characteristics, as affirmed even by his enemies. In addition, hundreds of miracles were done through his hands, such as quenching an army's thirst with water flowing from his fingers, splitting the moon with a gesture (*and the moon split* [54:1]), and causing many soldiers to flee by tossing a handful of soil at them (*It was not you who threw when you threw, but God threw* [8:17]). Learning of, or even witnessing them, the traveler says to himself: "One who performs such clear miracles to demonstrate and possesses such moral qualities and perfections must be the most truthful in speech. How could he ever lower himself to lies and trickery, which are vices of the vile?"

SECOND: He holds the decree of the universe's Owner (the Qur'an), which has been accepted and affirmed in every century by hundreds of millions of people and is miraculous in seven ways and 40 aspects. The traveler thinks: "The translator, expounder, and proclaimer of such a Decree of pure truth could not lie, for that would violate the Decree and betray the Owner."

THIRD: The like of the Sacred Law, religion, code of worship, way of prayer, message, and belief that he brought has never existed before. Nor could it exist (without him). The unequaled law brought by the unlettered Prophet has administered one-fifth of humanity for 14 centuries in a just and precise manner. Islam, which originated in and is represented by the Prophet's sayings, precepts, and example, is also peerless.

It has served hundreds of millions of people, regardless of time and place, as a guide and competent authority or source to decide every issue perfectly. It has trained their minds, illumined and purified their hearts, trained and refined their souls, and perfected their spirits.

The Prophet is the foremost practitioner of the worship prescribed by Islam and the most God-conscious person. He worshipped with the utmost care and attention to even the minutest details, even during times of great peril and throughout a life of constant struggle and activity. He imitated no one in his worship, and perfectly combined the beginning and end of spiritual evolution.

His prayers and knowledge of God are unparalleled, for with just the *Jawshan al-Kabir*, one of his thousands of supplicatory prayers, he describes his Lord with such a degree of knowledge that all saints and others foremost in knowledge of God since his time have never achieved a similar degree, despite their building upon their predecessors' accomplishments. Those who glance at just one of this supplication's 99 sections concludes that there can never be another one even remotely like it.

While preaching and calling his people to the truth, the Prophet displayed such steadfastness, firmness, and courage that he never faltered or hesitated. And this was despite the surrounding powers' and religions' hostility, as well as that of his own people, tribe, and even his uncle. He successfully challenged the world, thereby making Islam superior to all other religions and systems. This proves that no other person can equal him in his preaching of and calling humanity to the message of Truth.

His belief was so extraordinarily strong and certain, so miraculously evolved[298] (developed, expanded, and ingrained in his heart), and so elevated and world-enlightening that no prevailing ideas and beliefs, philosophies or spiritual teachings engendered any doubt within him. Despite their opposition and hostility, they could not make him hesitate or become anxious about his cause.

---

[298] We first believe in something's truth via simple acceptance or study and confirmation. As we learn the content of that in which we profess belief and experience belief's taste, our belief becomes stronger and more ingrained in our hearts. We can consider this an expansion, development, or deepening in confirmation. The Prophet went through this same procedure for, like every other believer, he evolved spiritually in his own realm: Prophethood. (Tr.)

Moreover all saints (primarily his Companions) have benefited—and continue to do so—from his faith, which they admit to be of the highest degree. This proves that his belief is matchless. The traveler seeking God thus concludes that lying and deception have no place in the person who brought such a unique law and matchless religion; who displayed such wonderful worship, extra-ordinary excellence in prayer, and world-admired preaching; and who possessed a belief of such miraculous perfection.

FOURTH: The Prophets' consensus is a very strong proof of God's Existence and Oneness and a firm testimony to that exalted person's truthfulness and Messengership. Even history confirms that he possessed to the utmost degree all of the sacred attributes, miracles, and functions that indicate a Prophet's truthfulness and Messengership.

The Prophets verbally predicted his coming by giving good tidings of him in the Torah, Gospels, Psalms, and Pages. Their missions and miracles affirmed and "put their signature" on the mission of this foremost and most perfect person's Prophethood. The traveler perceives that all of the previous Prophets bear witness to this person's truthfulness through the unanimity of their actions, just as they testify to God's Oneness through verbal consensus.

FIFTH: Having attained truth, perfection, the rank of working wonders, insight into the reality of things, and spiritual discovery by following that person's deeds and principles, thousands of saints bear witness to God's Oneness and that person's truthfulness and Messengership. The traveler realizes that they testify to that person's truthfulness, which is as bright as the sun; that they witness, through the light of sainthood, some of the truths he proclaimed about the Unseen world; and that they believe in and affirm all of those truths through the light of belief to the degree of certainty by knowledge, certainty by sight, or certainty by experience.

SIXTH: Thousands of exacting pure scholars, meticulous truthful scholars, and believing sages, all of whom reached the highest station of learning through the teaching contained in the sacred truths brought by that unlettered person; the sublime sciences to which he gave birth; and the knowledge of God he discovered—all prove and affirm God's Oneness, his mission's foundation, and bear witness to that greatest teacher's and supreme master's truthfulness and to the truth of his words.

SEVENTH: After the Prophets, his Family and Companions are the most renowned, respected, celebrated, pious, and keen-sighted members of humanity. Such a distinction is due to their insight, wisdom, and spiritual accomplishments. Having thoroughly examined and scrutinized all of the Prophet's thoughts, they concluded unanimously that he was the most truthful, elevated, and honest person in the world. The traveler understands that such an unshakable affirmation of and firm belief in him from such extraordinary people proves the truth of his cause, just as daylight proves the sun's existence.

EIGHTH: This universe indicates the Maker, Inscriber, and Designer Who has made it a palace, an exhibition, and a spectacle. Thus there should be a truthful unveiler who discovers the Divine purpose for the universe's creation, an exalted herald who announces this great book's meaning, and a discerning master and truthful teacher who teaches Divine Wisdom. He also should teach the meaning and outcome of the universe's transformations and purposeful motions.

The traveler gradually realizes that the one carrying out such duties most perfectly is the most truthful in his cause: serving as the Creator of the universe's most exalted and trusted officer.

NINTH: Behind the veil of creation is One Who wills, through these purposeful and skilled works, to display His perfect skills and art; to make Himself known and loved through those countless adorned creatures; to evoke praise and thanksgiving in return for His boundless invaluable bounties; and to encourage worship with gratitude and appreciation for His Lordship by means of His affectionate and protective sustenance of life, as well as His satisfying all things' varied tastes and appetites.

He wills to show His Divinity via the creativity and purposeful activity shown during the changing of seasons and the alternation of day and night, for example, so that humanity might believe in, submit to, and obey His Divinity. He wills to show His justice and truthfulness by protecting virtue and the virtuous and destroying evil and the evil, by annihilating oppressors and liars with heavenly blows.

Certainly the most beloved who, serving the Divine purpose to the highest degree, discloses creation's mystery, always acts in the name of that Being (his Creator), and asks Him alone for help and success (and receives both), will be with Him. This is Prophet Muhammad.

The traveler tells his reason: "Since these nine truths testify to that person's truthfulness, he must be the source of humanity's honor and the world's pride. Therefore he is worthy of being called 'the pride of the world' and 'the glory of humanity.'" Moreover the Qur'an, the All-Compassionate's miraculous exposition and Decree that he holds in his hand, has gathered half of the world into its magnificent spiritual domain. Together with the Messenger's personal perfections and elevated virtues, it shows that he is the most important being in the world, and accordingly, that his words about our Creator are the most important.

Come now and see! His sole cause was to prove and bear witness to the Necessarily Existent Being's Existence and Oneness, to proclaim Him with all His Attributes and Names. Based on the strength of his hundreds of miracles and the thousands of sublime, established truths contained in his religion, He is the "spiritual sun" enlightening the world, our Creator's most brilliant proof, the "Beloved of God." Each of the following three forms of great, truthful, and unshakable consensus affirms and corroborates the witness that he bears:

FIRST: The unanimous confirmation of that illustrious community known and celebrated as Muhammad's Family and descendants, among whom are thousands of spiritual poles and supreme saints of such keen sight as to penetrate into the Unseen, like Imam 'Ali, who said: "Were the veil lifted from the Unseen, my certainty would not increase," and 'Abd al-Qadir al-Jilani, who "saw" God's Mighty Throne and Archangel Israfil's awesome form while still alive.

SECOND: The unanimous confirmation of the Companions, made with so strong a belief that they sacrificed their lives and properties, their parents and tribes for its sake. Although brought up among a primitive people and in a climate of ignorance devoid of any positive notions of social life and administration, without any Scripture and immersed in the darkness of the uncivilized era after the Prophets, these people began to follow the Prophet's footsteps and soon became the masters, guides, and just rulers of the most civilized and socially and politically advanced peoples and states.

THIRD: The unanimous confirmation, made with the certainty of knowledge, by innumerable exacting and profound scholars. Each century has seen thousands of such people who became extraordinarily advanced in each branch of science and art.

Thus that person's testimony to God's Existence and Unity is so universal and unshakable that even if all beings hostile to it united, they still could not challenge it. Such is the conclusion reached by the traveler. In reference to the lesson learned in the School of Light while mentally visiting the Age of Happiness, we conclude: There is no deity but God, the Necessarily Existent Being, the One and Unique, the necessity of Whose Existence in Unity is clearly demonstrated by the pride of the world and the glory of humanity, through the majesty of the Qur'an's sovereignty, the splendor of Islam's inclusiveness, his perfections' multiplicity, and his moral qualities' sublimity as confirmed even by his enemies.

Again, he bears witness and brings proof through the strength of his hundreds of miracles that prove his truthfulness and are established firmly; and through the strength of thousands of evident and decisive truths contained in Islam, as affirmed by the consensus of his illustrious, enlightened Family and descendants disseminating lights, and the agreement of his Companions with penetrating sight and prudence, and the concord all of his community's scholars with enlightening proofs and insight.

Index

A

Abraham (Prophet), 159, 168, 170

Abu Bakr, 11, 24, 27, 30, 36, 41, 43, 56, 57, 65, 77, 91, 93, 95, 125, 126, 130, 138, 144, 145, 148, 234

Abu Jahl, 11, 31, 106, 144, 147, 234

Adam (Prophet), 220

Age of Happiness, 256

Ahl al-Sunna wa al-Jama'a, 39

angels, 130, 136, 139, 141, 143, 151, 182, 201, 207, 214, 241

animals, 9, 10, 75, 126, 130, 136, 177, 215

Arabic, 1, 190, 199, 245

Ascension, 22, 186, 224, 236, 238, 242, 244

B

belief, 4, 10, 22, 23, 28, 46, 69, 90, 140, 172, 187, 192, 201, 202, 203, 205, 208, 213, 233, 236, 243, 247, 249, 251, 252, 255

Bible, 151, 158, 159, 164, 168

Book of the Universe, 212, 225, 228

C

causality, 39

cause, 20, 24, 111, 152, 190, 204, 208, 215, 220, 235, 237, 244, 249, 252, 253, 254

cause and effect, 235

chance, 77, 191, 215

Children of Israel, 169

Chosroes, 43, 44, 119, 176, 180, 239

Christianity, 170

Christians, 39, 152, 153, 157, 159, 170

civilization, 29, 151, 231

Companions, 2, 10, 18, 19, 22, 25, 28, 30, 31, 35, 39, 42, 43, 46, 47, 53, 55, 57, 61, 68, 69, 70, 72, 80, 86, 88, 91, 92, 100, 103, 114, 115, 125, 131, 133, 139, 140, 141, 164, 186, 230, 235, 250, 252, 255, 257

compassion, 18, 207

conflict, 25
conscience, 199, 202
consciousness, 5
contentment, 143, 211
contingency, 244
corruption, 32, 152, 154, 171, 238
creation, 8, 9, 20, 65, 68, 150, 184, 185, 193, 194, 204, 206, 208, 214, 215, 220, 221, 228, 240, 242, 246, 252, 253, 254

D

David (Prophet), 160, 166
Day of Judgment, 89, 167, 230
Day of Resurrection, 96
death, 9, 18, 24, 25, 27, 30, 35, 37, 51, 102, 113, 165, 191, 214, 230
desire, 3, 25, 81, 190, 221
despair, 17
Destiny, 39
destruction, 34, 120, 152
deviation, 191, 192
disease, 112

E

Egypt, 27, 154, 192
enjoyment, 241

eternal life, 111, 222
eternity, 200, 211, 242
evil, 23, 34, 39, 51, 160, 161, 217, 253
evolution, 248
Existence (Divine), 204, 212, 246, 250, 254, 256

F

falsehood, 53, 97, 114, 152, 158, 169, 170, 183
fear, 19, 95, 96, 133
free will, 11, 39, 233
future, 10, 17, 18, 22, 36, 49, 126, 155, 169, 175, 189, 200, 213, 218, 219

G

Gabriel (Archangel), 20, 22, 81, 94, 139, 140, 141, 167, 202, 207
generosity, 116
Gnostics, 171, 175
goodness, 166, 203
Gospels, 153, 155, 158, 162, 170, 171, 213, 223, 238, 250
grace, 54, 230
gratitude, 253
grave, 22, 121, 138, 178, 203, 230

Greece, 157, 158

guidance, 4, 35, 199, 201, 202, 205, 214, 216, 220, 223, 228, 235

H

happiness, 6, 11, 36, 199, 201, 203, 204, 205, 206, 208, 216, 219, 220, 222, 242, 246

harmony, 166, 204

heart, 10, 52, 190, 198, 199, 202, 210, 237, 249

heavens, 68, 96, 186, 194, 219, 220, 221, 225, 232, 237, 244

heedlessness, 173

Hell, 13

Hereafter, 111, 167, 184, 189, 193, 196, 203, 225

heretics, 54

I

idols, 97, 177, 178, 180, 239

ignorance, 234, 255

illusion, 213

imagination, 201, 214, 245

insight, 12, 13, 36, 202, 251, 252, 257

inspiration, 12, 25, 173, 175, 191, 236

intellect, 199, 215, 246

intuition, 96, 201

Israfil (Archangel), 255

J

Jesus (Prophet), 39, 40, 112, 154, 159, 162, 163, 169, 170, 171, 174, 192

Jews, 40, 63, 100, 122, 150, 152, 153, 156, 160, 171

jinn, 85, 130, 136, 139, 141, 142, 143, 175, 177, 183, 184, 193, 194, 196, 197, 201, 204, 207, 208, 209, 214, 224, 241

jurisprudence, 54, 84

justice, 19, 164, 213, 235, 253

K

knowledge, 5, 18, 24, 38, 107, 175, 183, 189, 193, 194, 198, 201, 203, 205, 207, 211, 225, 228, 229, 230, 237, 248, 251, 256

L

law, 164, 171, 201, 225, 235, 239, 247, 250

life, 11, 66, 92, 102, 103, 123, 161, 175, 194, 201, 207, 210, 211, 214, 230, 248, 253 light, 5, 8, 28, 101, 118, 141, 143, 151, 179, 199, 201, 202, 203, 208, 214, 215, 216, 223, 230, 246, 251

love, 6, 19, 39, 40, 41, 89, 90, 96, 207, 216, 240, 243

M

Madina, 37, 43, 44, 47, 60, 95, 111, 122, 124, 125, 130, 134, 135, 144, 155, 212

Magians, 39, 180

Mahdi, 17, 18

Makka, 30, 33, 43, 44, 45, 93, 97, 131, 133, 145, 149, 156, 162, 163, 170, 177, 180, 181, 212

martyr, 138

martyrdom, 95, 138

matter, 16, 17, 19, 134, 230

memory, 1, 2, 65, 66

mercy, 20, 32, 105, 216, 221, 224, 229, 230

Messengership, 2, 3, 8, 13, 20, 87, 139, 151, 163, 172, 175, 177, 178, 203, 205, 218, 222, 223, 234, 235, 236, 237, 242, 244, 250, 251

Michael (Archangel), 20, 141

mind, 4, 13, 52, 111, 149, 192, 233, 235

miracle, 6, 11, 16, 24, 41, 46, 52, 56, 61, 62, 64, 65, 66, 67, 69, 70, 72, 73, 76, 77, 79, 80, 82, 85, 87, 91, 101, 102, 110, 118, 125, 128, 129, 133, 141, 143, 185, 188, 189, 191, 197, 202, 224, 231, 232, 233, 234, 235, 236

misfortune, 187

morality, 4, 5, 206

Moses (Prophet), 73, 101, 102, 160, 161, 162, 163, 192, 226

Musaylima, 47, 195

N

nature, 5, 19, 20, 21, 69, 129, 189, 199, 202, 235, 238

necessity, 201, 256

neediness, 215

O

order, 7, 10, 27, 52, 66, 85, 111, 135, 187, 209, 220, 222, 229, 239, 245

P

Paraclete, 158, 159, 169

Paradise, 21, 52, 89, 95, 103, 115, 117, 132, 140, 199, 203, 222, 230, 244

past, 48, 126, 189, 193, 194, 200, 213

People of the Book, 152

philosophy, 202, 228, 229

piety, 19, 26, 211

pity, 136, 165

pleasure, 137

poetry, 193

polytheism, 167

prayer, 7, 15, 16, 45, 71, 72, 95, 108, 110, 112, 115, 116, 117, 118, 121, 122, 124, 129, 147, 212, 220, 222, 224, 225, 247, 250

property, 194, 218

Prophethood, 5, 6, 7, 9, 10, 11, 14, 20, 32, 37, 38, 40, 67, 68, 69, 78, 85, 90, 94, 97, 98, 130, 133, 135, 138, 141, 151, 152, 154, 155, 163, 173, 174, 175, 176, 181, 182, 184, 185, 188, 205, 206, 223, 225, 231, 233, 235, 238, 249, 250

Prophets, 10, 98, 151, 167, 168, 170, 171, 199, 204, 212, 213, 233, 236, 250, 252, 255

purity, 29, 143, 171, 201, 202, 205

purpose, 19, 43, 67, 72, 127, 184, 208, 214, 221, 227, 233, 241, 252, 254

Q
R

Rafidites, 40, 41

reality, 7, 9, 17, 194, 217, 227, 229, 236, 251

reason, 25, 91, 147, 152, 231, 235, 238, 254

reasoning, 200, 202

rebellion, 23

reflection, 198, 207

religion, 4, 38, 114, 140, 143, 166, 171, 176, 193, 194, 196, 205, 206, 208, 209, 227, 233, 240, 247, 250, 255

Resurrection, 220, 226

Revelation, 13, 17, 173, 174, 183, 199, 200, 201, 218, 224

reward, 47, 70, 144, 244

righteousness, 166, 170, 206

Risala al-Hamidiya, 154, 159, 238

Risale-i Nur, 237

S

sainthood, 26, 189, 201, 236, 237, 251

saints, 18, 24, 26, 27, 29, 38, 170, 171, 199, 205, 212, 213, 224, 225, 248, 250, 251, 255

Satan, 62, 101, 144, 189

science, 103, 107, 198, 228, 229, 231, 256

Scriptures, 151, 152, 154, 155, 172, 173, 213

season, 192

separation, 88, 89, 214

service, 175

Shari'a, 16, 28, 90, 107, 185, 189, 205, 213

sin, 22, 166

sincerity, 90, 206, 211, 218

social life, 227, 255

soul, 22, 84

spirit, 159, 207, 226, 230, 234

submission, 94

Sufyan, 45, 132, 133, 141

Sunna, 32, 39, 90

Suyuti, 42, 141, 142, 177, 180, 182

T

theologians, 202, 236

Torah, 151, 152, 153, 155, 156, 158, 159, 160, 161, 162, 163, 168, 169, 171, 213, 223, 238, 250

transgression, 40

transience, 242

Truth, 97, 160, 208, 223, 230, 249

tyranny, 32

U

ugliness, 222

unbelief, 201

Unity (Divine), 204, 205, 212, 213, 226, 240, 242, 244, 256

V

vicegerent, 215

virtue, 26, 140, 202, 208, 253

W

weakness, 215

wisdom, 5, 196, 215, 225, 240, 244, 252

worship, 4, 213, 222, 225, 237, 240, 242, 247, 248, 250, 253

X

Y

Z